Strategic Planning Management

A Roadmap to Success

David I. Bertocci

University Press of America,® Inc.

Lanham · Boulder · New York · Toronto · Plymouth, UK

Copyright © 2009 by
University Press of America,® Inc.
4501 Forbes Boulevard
Suite 200
Lanham, Maryland 20706
UPA Acquisitions Department (301) 459-3366

Estover Road
Plymouth PL6 7PY
United Kingdom

Library of Congress Control Number: 2009922991
ISBN-13: 978-0-7618-4590-4 (paperback : alk. paper)
eISBN-13: 978-0-7618-4591-1

Contents

Contents

Preface

Strategic Planning and Management: A Roadmap to Success is the second in a series of three books written by Dr. Bertocci primarily for distance-learning students in online undergraduate and graduate programs with a focus on strategic planning and management, leadership in organizations and organizational structures and development. While the books are intended primarily for online, distance-learning students, they also have applicability in the traditional classroom.

The first book introduced concepts of leadership and leadership theories and principles across a broad spectrum. This second book focuses on strategic planning and management in organizations and presents a unique perspective on development of the strategic plan. It approaches the subject from a participatory management perspective featuring development of the strategic plan by a team of employees spanning the organization chart. A significant theme of the book is the hands-on approach to strategic planning and management that includes the underlying theory and principles as well as the step by step process of developing the strategic plan. The book has two purposes. The first purpose was as stated above and was strictly academic. However, since most distance-education students are working adults who may actually be called upon to participate in the strategic planning process or even to lead a strategic planning team, the secondary purpose was to present a step-by-step list of actions to develop an organization's strategic plan.

Online Distance Education

While there are numerous textbooks, academic papers and other scholarly documents written relative to strategic planning and management, most are not written with online distance-learning students in mind and in many cases concentrate on only a few of the principles of strategic planning and management. By contrast, this book has two distinct parts: the first, introducing the student to underlying theory and principles of planning and development of the strategic plan, and the second, providing a step-by-step process for developing an organization's strategic plan.

In several respects, online students are unlike students in a traditional college campus setting. Most online students are working adults with full-time or part-time jobs, growing families and endless responsibilities that demand their time and compete for their attention. Yet they have the motivation and desire to learn and advance their education. As busy adults, they need textbooks that not only contain the necessary material, are clearly written and easy to read, but also are engaging and stimulating.

As I discovered during my own online education—and while teaching online courses for over twelve years—online distance education is challenging. Typically there is no professor in front of a classroom explaining, describing, and defining the text material. This leaves the online student to comprehend it all without the benefit of in-depth classroom discussion. Having obtained both my masters and doctoral degrees in a distance-learning program as a mature adult with a full-time job, growing family, dependent parents, and other demanding obligations, I found that very few textbooks satisfied my needs.

Textbooks for online education must be clearly written at an appropriate academic level, must maintain academic rigor and must present the material in an appropriate structure and format so that students can understand it without the benefit of direct classroom participation. Thus, this book is written primarily for students in online distance-learning programs, working adults who may be called upon to participate in the strategic planning process or even be called on by their organization to lead a planning team. It addresses a need for textbooks that are both engaging and specifically designed to meet these criteria. Although the primary purpose for this book is use in the distance-learning environment, it may also be used in traditional university classrooms, especially at the undergraduate level.

In addition to my online graduate coursework and research, and my experience teaching online undergraduate and graduate courses, I bring to this book many years of hands-on planning and management experience from a number of work situations in the military and in industry. Thus, the selection and syntheses of the literature cited in this book reflect a real-world view of planning and management theory and principles based upon direct experience.

Overview of the Text

The material in this book is organized in two parts and is designed so the student will gain basic information from the early chapters. Part One discusses strategic planning and management by looking first at the underlying theory and principles of planning across a broad spectrum and their application to the strategic process. Then two of the prominent planning tools are examined in depth: the Organizational System Analysis and the Skills, Weakness, Opportunities, and Threats (SWOT) process. The student is presented with a variety of internal and external assessments that affect the final strategic plan. My bringing relevant and meaningful data from recognized authors and experts in the subject matter, gives the student access to an overview of theory and principles from several different perspectives.

Part Two concentrates on the actual planning process: selection of the planning team; the role of top management; procedures for setting the vision; the need for clear mission statements; and setting strategic goals with specific tactical objectives, including the timeframes for each. Students can see that the planning process is a step-by-step, systematic process that is used to develop the actual strategic plan.

Strategic Planning and Management: A Roadmap to Success is designed not only to convey a real-world view of meaningful strategic planning theory, but also to encourage students to compare and contrast real-world situations with the planning theories presented in the book. In doing so, management and business students learn to recognize the dynamics of strategic planning in operational situations and can begin to apply strategic planning principles in working situations.

David I. Bertocci, Ph.D.

Acknowledgments

Putting together a manuscript for publication is a monumental task and certainly not an individual effort. There are many people who contribute to getting even one book published; but getting three textbooks written, edited, and published is almost impossible without the help of many family members, associates, and friends. There is no way I can personally thank the many people who have helped me along the way; but there are a few who deserve special recognition.

First, I would like to recognize Dr. Jay Avella, my mentor during my doctoral studies. Jay first saw something in my work and then planted the seed that perhaps some of the doctoral research could eventually be published. I have him to thank for getting me thinking about publishing my manuscripts.

Second, although I take full responsibility for the contents of this book, I thank my editor for taking my random notes, disjointed sentences and unfocused paragraphs and turning them into what you read between these covers. My editor had monumental patience with me but continued to press me to finish or else, like many engineers, I would engineer the thing to death, always trying to get to the one hundred percent solution.

Lastly, I thank my wife Nancy for her patience with me these nearly fifty years. I moved her all over the world, left her and our children for foreign deployments, and generally became difficult to manage as the years went on. I cannot thank her enough for giving up her career and following mine; for warming up dinner many times when I was stuck behind the computer; and for excusing me when I could not attend something she wanted to do all because I was trying to gather my thoughts and finish a chapter or two.

Introduction

O f the many challenges faced by leaders and managers, managing change is one of the most difficult. One of the reasons strategic planning and management has become so important in recent years is that the business world has become more competitive and more volatile. Changes in organizational design, structure and leadership are needed for survival in this new environment. Companies reorganize to eliminate unneeded and unwanted operations and/or absorb smaller companies through mergers and acquisitions. As organizational changes are implemented, tensions generated by new relationships are inevitable. Thus, before we can address how change in organizations can be accomplished effectively, we must first examine factors that affect change in organizations, types of change within an organization, strategies to manage change in an organization, and how leaders and managers differ in dealing with change.

The Changing Environment

Business has changed dramatically in recent decades and continues to change, even as you are reading this publication. Global competition, worldwide markets, new technologies, and the significantly different global workforce, have forced companies to become more aware of who they are, where they are with respect to their competition, where they want to go in the marketplace, and how they are going to get there. Mergers, acquisitions, global competition, foreign workforces, and demands for new worker benefits are all common in today's news.

The increase in competition is simply too severe for organizations to continue to operate without changing in order to stay competitive with other organizations that have already adapted to these global conditions. Each organization must become able to compete globally, reduce costs, invigorate the workforce, and survive in today's merger and acquisition arena. Companies that were once thought to be invulnerable no longer exist, having been bought out by other companies only to be merged or acquired by yet others. Organizations come into existence only to disappear a few years later when a new organization is created by a merger or acquisition. In the name of increased efficiency, these continual changes seek to streamline or improve the organization or simply eliminate unneeded and unwanted operations. Personnel billets to staff these organizations are passed from the original organization to the new one, and organizational codes disappear and reappear, resulting in a new organization that is not very much more efficient than the old one. Montana suggests that the more things change, the more they stay the same, no change is final, and a course of action that needs no further adjustment is impossible to achieve.[1] Montana describes change in the organization as a process of transforming the way in which an organization acts from one set of behaviors to another, which may either be planned or be implemented in a random manner.[2] George and Jones describe organizational change as the movement of an organization away from its present state toward some desired future state to increase its effectiveness.[3]

The workplace, whether it is in industry, government, or non-profit organizations, is continually changing. Gibson, Ivancevich and Donnelly theorize that the workplace will change even more dramatically in the next few years.[4] According to their research, the average company grew in size up to the 1990s, and some companies continue to grow today. However, many companies have become smaller, especially in manufacturing or production industries through mergers, acquisitions, downsizing, reengineering and other streamlining processes as bits and pieces of their industry are sold off. In *Straight from the Gut*, Jack Welch describes this process as parts of GE were sold off during his tenure as CEO of General Electric.[5]

Certainly, the global marketplace and changes in the way companies do business are factors too. Customers are always looking for better, cheaper, faster goods and services. The rise in technological advancements is also a factor, as technology has eliminated many routine jobs. Businesses are also increasingly outsourcing to suppliers and subcontractors many tasks once performed in-house. There are many reasons companies change their organizational structure and the list provided above hardly covers the entire spectrum. The point is that organizations are changing all the time and these structural changes impact employees, managers and corporate executives. Thus, leaders and managers need to have both training and experience in implementing changes in an organization as well as dealing with and minimizing the impact on employees of changes in the organizational structure within the company.

Reasons for Change

There are many reasons for change in organizations, some of them external to the organization and some internal.[6] External factors that bring about the need to change include the need for different goods and services, changes in laws or regulations pertaining to the business, different customer requirements, changes in pricing structures, new competition as a result of a merger or acquisition, new business opportunities, and other changes in the marketplace. External factors also include economic forces that are at play worldwide, *e.g.*, the North American Free Trade Agreement (NAFTA), emergence of the European Union, and political forces that are constantly evolving both in the United States and globally.

Internal forces that create change within an organization include the need for a different organizational structure to accommodate changes in the business, realignment of lines of control, and different human resource requirements. Other internal factors are an increase in foreign and female employees creating a demand for benefits and perks not seen before, and changes in ethical standards as a consequence of business scandals, such as that which occurred in the case of Enron Corporation.

With the emergence of a global marketplace, organizations can no longer look only within the boundaries of the United States for competition or for their product sales. Increased diversity of the workforce with more foreign-born workers and an increase in female workers has forced companies to consider childcare facilities, elder care facilities, union demands, flexible work schedules, and benefits not seen before.

Researcher Kurt Lewin developed the force field theory regarding organizational change, which hypothesizes that organizational change occurs when forces for change strengthen, resistance to change lessens, or both occur simultaneously.[7] According to the force field theory, there are always two sets of forces in an organization—the force to change and the force to remain as is. If both forces are balanced, the organization is in a state of inertia and managers must find a way to overcome this inertia if an organization is to change.

Managing Change Strategically

When we talk about change in an organization, we are talking both about changes that affect people, and how leaders and managers bring those changes about. Some organizations resist the need to change and can never seem to get out of the state of inertia; yet others change almost constantly, never experiencing inertia. In many cases, to compensate for these dramatic changes in the marketplace, organizations modify their organizational structures. Some downsize their workforces and many outsource their routine functions in an effort to be more competitive. Some of the more significant changes in the workplace include revising or eliminating traditional organizational structures, reducing or eliminating middle layers of management, consolidating workforces, increasing interest in alliances, in mergers, and in acquisitions, globalizing operations, and increasing emphasis on reducing operating costs by reducing employee benefits and perks.

In the face of this rapidly changing internal and external environment, leaders and managers of successful organizations understand several factors 1) change in the organization is necessary to keep pace with the competition, to streamline operations and to reduce operating costs 2) the marketplace is becoming more global and the organization must adapt to these changing conditions 3) the workforce has certain needs and wants that must be considered in any changes to the organization structure and 4) any change in the organization requires careful and resolute planning, communication, and implementation. More than ever, leaders and managers of successful companies have a keen awareness of the importance of successfully managing change in the workplace.

Evidence of this increased awareness of the changing business world can be seen in the renewed interest in strategic management courses by working adults who see these changes first hand. In the business environment, some workers may be called upon to lead or participate in the planning process, while others may have even been personally affected by these changes in the form of reduction or elimination of their jobs.

In some form or another, strategic management is being practiced at all levels and in all organizations. Surely, even the builders of the great pyramids had some form of overall master plan. In today's rapidly changing business environment, larger companies are repeatedly acquiring smaller companies. This seems to be an attempt to increase their capabilities while at the same time reduce the workforce by combining groups, sections and departments. In some industries, there are very few companies still in existence as they were before, with the end result being reduction of the number of companies in the marketplace. Surviving companies have more capabilities and are doing more with less. With the global economy powered by the Internet, it becomes even more critical for companies to have a strategic plan to follow. Many business experts would agree that without a strategic plan, companies are like a drifting, rudderless boat.[8]

There are several key advantages to following the strategic planning and management process outlined in this book. 1) The planning team, comprised of workers and managers throughout the organization can use their wide range of expertise and experience. 2) Involvement by top management in setting a strategic vision clarifies where the organization is, where it is going and how it is going to get there. 3) Their active participation in the planning process makes that vision acceptable to the workforce. 4) Managers and workers cooperate in setting the direction of the company. 5) There is more willingness to accept redistribution of scarce financial and personnel resources to support the planning process. 6) A more proactive management posture is created. It has been repeatedly demonstrated that successful organizations use strategic planning to guide their business conduct and to help make deliberate, rational, choices among alternative courses of action. Without an over-riding strategy the organization will not have a clear direction to follow and no unified program to produce management's intended results.

Summary

There should no longer be any doubt that the business environment continues to change rapidly. Just look at the business section of your local newspaper. Mergers, acquisitions, global competition, foreign workforces are all very visible in today's news. Surely, managers today must think strategically about their business enterprise. It has been well documented by researchers, that to survive in this evolving marketplace, it is essential that managers know their organization well enough to compare their capabilities to others in the global economy. It is also essential that they have some form of overall strategic plan for the organization to follow. This implies an in-depth understanding of the internal and external forces that impact the organization and its resources. Managers must also be aware of external factors such as changing customer requirements, foreign competition, and mergers and acquisitions of companies within their industry in order to know when to institute strategic changes. An examination of the internal operations and processes of the business determines what kinds of strategic changes will be most effective for the company.

Strategic planning is not only beneficial, but essential for any size business or organization to survive in the global economy. Organizational leaders have to think strategically about their company's position and the impact of changing conditions; they have to know the business well enough to know what kinds of strategic changes to initiate; and they have to monitor the external situation closely enough to know when to institute them. Strategic management drives the whole approach to managing an organization. A comprehenive strategic planning process gives the business manager/owner a perspective of the company not found in other managerial or operational processes. Through the Organization System Analysis (or a formal SWOT Process), the strategic planner conducts an in-depth review of the company's strengths, weaknesses, and opportunities, as well as a thorough analysis of the roadblocks that limit achievement of the vision.

Notes

1. Patrick J. Montana and Bruce H. Charnov, *Management*, 3d ed., (New York: Barron's Management Series, 1992), 348.

2. Montana, 348.

3. Jennifer George and Gareth Jones, *Understanding and Managing Organizational Behavior*, 4th ed., (Upper Saddle River, NJ: Prentice Hall, 2004), 567.

4. James Gibson, John M. Ivancevich, and James H. Donnelly, *Organizations: Behavior, Structure, Processes: Behavior, Structure, Processes*, 10th ed.,(Boston: McGraw Hill-Irwin, 2002), 445.

5. Jack Welch and John A. Bryne, *Jack: Straight from the Gut*, (New York: Warner Business Books, 2001).

6. George and Jones, 567-70.

7. Kurt Lewin, *Field Theory in Social Science*, (New York: Harper & Row, 1951), cited by George and Jones, *Understanding,* 573.

8. Arthur A. Thompson, Jr. and A. J. Strickland III, *Strategic Management: Concepts and Cases,* 9th ed., (Chicago: Richard D. Irwin Company, 1996), 2.

Chapter 1

Theory and Perspective

Mary Coulter defines strategic planning as "a process of analyzing the current situation; developing appropriate strategies; putting those strategies into action; and evaluating, modifying or changing those strategies as needed."[1] Charles Hill and Gareth Jones describe strategic planning and management with four statements.[2]

1. Strategic leadership is about how to most effectively manage a company's strategy-making process to create competitive advantage.
2. In the strategy-making process managers select and then implement a set of strategies that aim to achieve a competitive advantage.
3. Strategy formulation is the task of selecting strategies.
4. Strategy implementation is the task of putting strategies into action which include designing, delivering and supporting products, improving the efficiency and effectiveness of operations; and designing a company's organization structure, control systems and culture.

Thompson and Strickland define strategic management as follows:

[S]trategic management refers to the managerial process of forming a strategic vision, setting objectives, crafting a strategy, implementing and executing the strategy, and then over time initiating whatever corrective adjustments in the vision, objectives, strategy, and execution are deemed appropriate.[3]

There is one more definition with which we open this chapter of the book.

Pearce and Robinson define strategic planning and management as the set of decisions and actions that result in the formulation and implementation of plans designed to achieve a company's objectives and are comprised of nine critical tasks.

1. Formulate the company's vision, mission, purpose, philosophy, and goals.
2. Conduct an analysis that reflects the company's internal and external capabilities.
3. Assess the company's external environment including competitive factors.
4. Analyze the company's options by matching resources with external environment.
5. Identify the most desirable options and evaluate against company mission.
6. Select a set of long term objectives and grand strategies.
7. Develop annual objectives and short term strategies that are compatible with the long term strategies and objectives.
8. Implement the strategic choices.
9. Evaluate the success of the process as input for future decision making.[4]

The definition of strategic planning and management developed by Pearce and Robinson provides a neat capsule of the strategic planning process addressed next. As you have already seen, different authors have different perspectives on strategic planning and management, but most agree with the overall concept that strategic thinking is the best way to change the organization from what is it today to what it needs to be tomorrow in order to compete in the constantly evolving business environment and marketplace.

Notice that some of the authors mentioned use the term *strategic management* and others, meaning the same thing, use the term *strategic leadership*. Other authors use the term *strategic planning* while still others use the term *long range planning*. In contrast, Montana defines long-range planning as the process of taking lower level organizational goals and objectives into account when developing long-range overriding strategic goals that support those shorter range actions that lead to the achievement of each strategic goal. Managers who embrace this planning philosophy think strategically about a company's situation and are astute at crafting and implementing their goals.[5]

Although all the definitions sound quite similar, research indicates that most practitioners of strategic planning and management define planning as 1) choosing a destination; 2) evaluating alternative routes; and 3) deciding on the specific course to reach the chosen destination. Planning then becomes an extremely important element of each manager's job since industry believes the cost of an error as a result of the old "seat of the pants" decision-making has become too expensive for today's complex economy. Formal, in-depth planning requires managers to sit down and think through issues and alternatives.

As we have seen, there are many meaningful definitions of strategic planning and management. Review of published material reveals that each author has a slightly different version of the definition. But one major theme running through most of the definitions is the perception that strategic management is a set of decisions and actions that result in the formulation (and implementation) of plans designed to achieve a company's long range objectives.

Researching material for this book found a consensus that strategic planning and management has several dimensions. Of course the depth and breadth of these factors directly relate to the size and complexity of the organization—the bigger and more complex the organization, the more complex the dimension of each area. Typically, strategic planners weigh multiple, inter-related issues.[6]

1. Strategic issues normally require top-management decisions.

By their very nature, strategic decisions impact multiple areas of a company's internal operations, involve major changes in direction of the company, or re sult in some other significant change in the business model. Typically these decisions require involvement of top managers with the overall perspective to understand their broad implications. Further, in most organizations, top management is vested with the power to authorize the necessary resource allocations. But as you will see, the need to involve other levels of the organization in the planning process is equally important. One of the principles set forth in the planning process outlined in Part 2 of this book is loosely based on one of the principles of "Total Quality Management" (TQM) inspired by the work of Dr. W. Edwards Deming. TQM has evolved over the years into the modern principle of participative management. One of its underlying hypotheses is that those charged with implementation of a plan should be involved in the planning process by being an integral part of the planning team.[7]

2. Strategic issues normally require large resources.

Strategic decisions and accomplishment of strategic goals involve substantial allocations of people, physical assets, and usually money—resoures that either must be redirected from internal sources or secured from outside the firm. Decisions reached as part of the strategic planning process often commit the company to actions over an extended period and therefore require substantial resources.

3. Strategic issues often affect the firm's long-term prosperity.

Strategic decisions by their very nature commit the company for a long time—typically five or more years. Once a company has committed itself to a particular strategy, its public image, its operating policies, and competitive advantages (or disadvantages) are tied to that strategy. Companies become known in certain markets, for certain products, with certain technologies. Consider Ford, GM, Microsoft, and Dell. These companies and many others would jeopardize their reputation and profitability if they shifted from their traditional markets, products, or technologies by adopting a radically different strategy. For instance, would the traditional auto industry do as well if they suddenly decided to switch from the car to the shoe business; or Dell to the bathroom tissue business? Obviously, strategic decisions can have enduring effects on firms for better or worse.

4. Strategic issues are future oriented.

Strategic decisions should be based on in-depth analysis of internal and external conditions, consideration of all-encompassing planning assumptions, identification of threats and roadblocks that impede achievement of the strategic vision, and other significant factors assessed during the planning process. This formal planning process places emphasis on the development of projections that will enable the firm to select the most promising strategic options—those that contribute to the company's competitive advantage in the marketplace. In a turbulent and highly competitive free enterprise environment, the company will survive only if it takes a pro-active stance toward change.

5. Strategic issues may affect multiple units in the company.

Strategic decisions have complex implications for most areas of the company. Decisions about such matters as customer mix, competitive emphasis, or organizational structure necessarily involve a number of the firm's strategic business units. Even in very small companies, these units will be affected by allocations or reallocations of responsibilities and resources that result from these decisions.

6. Strategic issues may affect external organizations or operations.

Companies are affected by both internal and external conditions; by customer demands; by changing marketplace conditions; and by strengths and weaknesses of employees, staff and management. Some of these conditions are largely outside of the companies' control. Therefore, to successfully position a firm in competitive situations, its strategic managers must look beyond its operations. They must consider what relevant competitors, customers, suppliers, creditors, government, and labor unions are likely to do.

As you will see, assumptions become important to the planning process, as well as consideration of a number of internal and external conditions. As any traveler understands, you must know where you are before you can chart a course to go where you want to be. Top level managers and leaders must assume that the competitors have previously engaged in their own strategic planning process giving them a competitive edge. Assume that the competition have already improved their productivity by focusing on achieving their vision, moving towards accomplishment of their strategic goals, and utilizing shared management. The organization must keep pace with them or be left in the dust. A challenge for all managers is the allocation of precious time and resources to conduct strategic planning in view of the many daily operational requirements. The old adage, "The spirit is willing but the body is weak," applies here. Even when managers are astute, forward-looking planners at the top of their game, the time and resources demanded by strategic planning may prove daunting. Nevertheless, inability—or unwillingness—to commit the time and resources necessary for such planning is potentially catastrophic.

Developing and implementing a strategy should be regarded as core management functions. Among a manager's functions, few affect company performance more fundamentally than how well its management team charts the company's long-term direction, develops competitively effective strategic business approaches, and executes the strategy in ways that produce the targeted results. Indeed, good strategy development and execution are the most evident signs of good management. Some managers design shrewd strategies, but fail to execute them well. Others design mediocre strategies, but execute them flawlessly. Both situations open the door to shortfalls in performance. Managers must combine good strategy making with good strategy execution for company performance to approach its maximum potential. The better conceived a company's strategy and the more proficient its execution, the greater the chance the company will be a solid performer. Matteson and Ivancevich provide an interesting perspective.[8] They indicate that planning is one of the functions recognized universally as central to managing. They point out that poor managers work on today's problems but good managers work on tomorrow's. Further they indicate that one of the major themes of the classical school of management is the distinct difference between managing and executing. Fayol and others argue that managers should be the ones to plan and execute while authorities in the behavioral school of management maintain that both managers and non-managers should participate in those processes.

In the small, growing business, strategic planning is even more important. A company's configuration changes as new markets are penetrated and new resources obtained. Additional personnel, each with different skills and attributes, present problems not faced earlier. For the small business owner, strategic planning and management is essential if the firm is to seize new business opportunities with unified vision and direction. This is not to say that the process for strategic planning is easy. In the small business, with its modest staff infrastructure, management is normally fully engaged and totally immersed in daily operations with very little time or opportunity to break away for strategic planning sessions.

Strategic planning for the small business should be the blueprint for strengthening the organization's position, pleasing customers, and improving overall performance levels. Even after careful planning the small business owner still faces the task of molding the decisions and competitive actions taken across the company into a cohesive pattern. Developing a sound strategic plan requires entrepreneurship and strategic thinking. Typically, small companies must keep their strategies closely matched to changing market situations and other outside influences. They must also exercise entrepreneurial skills by studying new market trends, listening to customers, enhancing the company competitiveness, and guiding the company activities into new directions in a timely manner. Appropriate strategy selection is essential to effective entrepreneurship. To be successful, a business, no matter what yardstick is used to measure success, must certainly know where it is in the marketplace, where it wants to go, and how it will get there. An organization's over-riding strategy consists of the actions and business approaches management employs to achieve the desired organizational performance.

As more and more companies move toward entrepreneurial operation in which middle and lower managers have a bigger part in the overall direction of the company, many benefits result from instilling a strategic planning and management mentality throughout the company.

1. Using the participatory management approach which holds that those charged with implementation of the final strategic plan should be part of the planning team, managers at all levels of the firm interact in planning and implementing. As a result, the behavioral consequences of strategic management are similar to those of participative decision making.
2. Strategy formulation activities enhance the firm's ability to prevent many problems. Managers at all levels who participate in the planning sessions are made acutely aware of the factors involved in that process. They become better at monitoring and forecasting and become even better managers.
3. Group-based strategic decisions are likely to be chosen from the best available alternatives. This type of strategic management process results in better decisions because group interaction generates a greater variety of alternative strategies. Also, forecasts based on the specialized perspectives of group members improve the screening of options. The involvement of employees in strategy formulation improves their understanding of the productivity-reward relationship in every strategic plan and, thus, reenforces their motivation.
4. Gaps and overlaps in activities among individuals and groups are reduced as participation in strategy formulation clarifies

differences in roles. Obviously, as middle managers become more aware of functions and activities in other parts of the company, they can work toward eliminating redundancies, gaps, and overlaps in functions and responsibilities in their own.

5. One of the major distractions in any organization is resistance to change. This resistance can be reduced simply by making sure that participants in the planning process understand the big picture—knowledge of where the company is, where they want to go, how they are going to get there and why. Because they are part of the planning process, their ownership of the plan reduces resistance to necessary changes.

Coulter describes strategic management in terms of four distinct characteristics. 1) Its interdisciplinary nature encompasses all aspects of the organization. 2) It facilitates interaction between the organization and the external environment; 3) It involves all elements of the organization's resources and capabilities. 4) It places major emphasis on the future direction of the organization.[9]

Characteristics of Strategic Management Planning and Management

Although the process may vary with the size and complexity of an organization, strategic planning and management has—according to a number of well-known researchers—several recognizable, distinguishing characteristics. Those presented here are only a sample of these many variations.[10]

1. The characteristics of strategic management decisions vary with the level of strategic activity considered. In other words, characteristics are different for different size organizations.
2. Decisions at the corporate level tend to be more global, more conceptual, and less concrete than decisions at subordinate, business, or functional levels. Corporate-level decisions are often characterized by greater risk, cost, and profit potential, greater need for flexibility; and longer time horizons. Such decisions tend to involve the over-riding direction of the company, its pursuit of varying business opportunities,

employment and other personal policies, and sources of its long-term financing, and priorities for its growth.

3. Functional-level decisions implement the overall strategy formulated at the corporate and business levels. They involve action-oriented operational issues and are relatively short-range and low risk. Functional-level decisions normally only incur modest costs and draw upon on existing resources. Because functional-level decisions are relatively concrete and quantifiable, they receive much critical attention and analysis even though their comparative profit potential is low.

4. Business-level decisions are associated with the lowest level of strategic decision making. Decisions reached at the business level are normally less costly, less risky, and potentially less profitable than corporate-level decisions. However, in certain instances the reverse can be true simply because they involve the product line—the primary concern of the organization.

Summary

As we have seen there are several perspectives on and definitions of strategic planning and management. Regardless of what the exact definition tends to be, one thing is clear: strategic planning and management is essential to successful management of the organization. With the global marketplace changing so dramatically and rapidly, an organization must have an overriding master plan to be followed both by top management and by the workforce. Together, management and workforce can do tremendous things, bringing success to the organization as it competes in the global marketplace. Divided, they will wander aimlessly, for the lack of shared vision and direction.

Notes

1. Mary Coulter, *Strategic Management in Action*, (Upper Saddle River, New Jersey: Pearson Education, 2005), 2-24.

2. Charles W. L. Hill and Gareth R. Jones, *Strategic Management Theory*, 7th ed., (Boston: Houghton Mifflin, 2007), 127-128.

3. Arthur A. Thompson, Jr. and A. J. Strickland III, *Strategic Management: Concepts and Cases*, 9th ed., (Chicago: Richard D. Irwin, 1996), 3.

4. John A. Pearce II and Richard B. Robinson, *Strategic Management,* (New York: McGraw Hill, 2007), 3.

5. Patrick J. Montana and Bruce H. Charnov, *Management*, 3d ed., (New York: Barron's Management Series, 3d ed., 2000), 120-122.

6. Pearce and Robinson, 4-5; Thompson and Strickland, 12th ed., 2-21; and Coulter, 2-24.

7. Mary Walton, *The Deming Management Method*, (New York: The Putnam Publishing Group, 1986), 33-34.

8. Michael T. Matteson and John M Ivancevich, eds., *Management and Organizational Behavior Classics,* 7th ed., (Boston: Irwin Mc Graw Hill, 1999), 67.

9. Coulter, 6.

10. Thompson and Strickland, 9th ed., 2-19.

Chapter 2

Real World Considerations

Strategy planning is a company's best game plan for strengthening its position, pleasing customers, and improving overall performance levels.[1] Famous for his management theories, Peter Drucker states, "Strategic management is not a box of tricks or a bundle of techniques. It is analytical thinking and commitment of resources to action."[2] If there is only one overriding reason to engage in strategic planning, it is to make the company more competitive and to increase profits. Make no mistake: companies exist to make money. Shareholders demand it, executive salaries require it, and employee compensation and rewards depend on it. Some companies may have esoteric and philosophical themes like making a better mousetrap, or providing better service to customers, but the underlying reason for the company to exist is to make a profit. No profits—no business; it's pure and simple!

In order to grasp the many aspects of strategic planning and management, you must first understand two fundamentals: what a business is and how it operates. These basics may seem obvious, but I have found that many people have misconceptions about what a business really is. Here is my simplified definition: a business is an organized effort of individuals to produce and sell goods and services for a profit. Businesses vary in size, as measured by number of employees or by sales volume. Large companies such as Exxon, Microsoft, or General Motors count their employees in the tens of thousands and their sales revenues in the billions. But most of the businesses in the United States are small, independently owned and operated, and have fewer than twenty employees. Whether a business has one employee working at home, several working in a retail store, many working in a plant or factory or even more working in branch offices nationwide, all commercial businesses share the same definition and are organized for the same purpose—to earn profits. Profit is the money that comes from a company's sale of goods and services, minus such costs of operation as salaries, benefits, and taxes. The majority of businesses in the United States are commercial enterprises, operating for a profit with income from sale of goods or services. Others businesses are non-profit operations that rely on income other than that from the sale of some product, service, or technical support.

The source of most business revenue, and therefore of profits, is sale of its goods and services. Goods are tangible items: products such as automobiles, shoes, radios, computers, and can openers. Services are intangibles, such as the professional advice and assistance provided by lawyers, doctors, accountants, electricians, and hairdressers. Technical support includes the services of consultants of many types, and others engaged in support activities for major enterprises.

Consumers will buy only those goods and services they need or want. Therefore, to be successful, businesses must provide goods and services that satisfy consumers' needs and wants. Consumers need and will buy shoes. Consumers may not *need* expensive high tech or exotic sport shoes, but they may purchase them if they *want* them. Therefore, identifying consumer needs and wants is key to business success. All goods and services are produced from five specific resources known as *factors of production*—land, labor, capital, information resources, and entrepreneurship.

So, with this little basic information from Business 101, we continue. If a firm's primary reason for existence is to make a profit, the challenge is to develop strategy-making procedures that produce strategies that will guide business decisions made, and competitive actions taken across the company, into a cohesive pattern that leads to increased profits. Since managerial decisions affect company performance (profits), how well the management team charts the company's long-term direction, develops competitively effective strategic business decisions, and executes that strategy in a timely manner, directly affects the bottom line. Indeed, good strategy *planning* and good strategy *execution* are identifiable signs of good management.[3]

Thompson and Strickland indicate five tasks normally performed by managers when conducting strategic planning and management for their organizations. These tasks are basic to the strategic plan.[4]

1. Deciding what business the company will actually be in, and then forming a strategic vision of where the organization is headed

   > These decisions give the organization its sense of purpose, provide long-term direction, and establish a clear mission. A well-conceived strategic vision is the basis for the future. It is the forward concept, developed by top management, modified by the planning team, and accepted by the workforce. It identifies a firm's long-term direction and states its determination to reach specific goals.

2. Converting that strategic vision and mission statement into measurable objectives, strategic goals, and tactical objectives
3. Converting all the gathered data into a strategic plan that will achieve the desired results
4. Implementing and executing the chosen strategy efficiently and effectively
5. Evaluating performance, reviewing new developments, and initiating corrective adjustments in long-term direction, goals, objectives, strategy, or implementation in light of actual experience, changing conditions, new ideas, and new opportunities

Although change will always be necessary—sooner or later—it often creates conflict within an organization. Employees tend to resist change for many reasons including fear of losing their jobs, uncertainty of what proposed changes will bring, and the discomfort of working with something unknown. But as one law of physics implies, "If something is not growing, it is dying." Inevitably, there is a need for changes to the organization's mission, structure, or operations, and they can be made successfully when they are carefully considered and thoroughly planned. Some organizations are constantly changing and never have a true identity. You know them! Perhaps you work for one of them. These are the companies that want to be something, want to go somewhere, and want to be known for something. The only problem is that they don't know how to get there. They don't know how to "pull the trigger" on strategic planning, or to carry out a strategic plan.

So, there are basic questions top management must ask before beginning the strategic planning process. Students of true strategic planning know that it is imperative, before embarking on this long journey, that the company's top management know where they are, where they want to go, and how they are going to get there.

Challenges

Industry leaders today face increasing levels of competition from all directions. There is no doubt that the marketplace has become global, with competition coming from all parts of the world. In spite of recent mergers and acquisitions, there seems to be more and more competition, as companies forming powerful alliances compete for the same markets. At best, it is a difficult task to compete with these new larger conglomerate companies. Economic conditions simply may not warrant investing large sums of capital in business development, and mergers with a larger company or acquisition of smaller ones cannot be executed. Large and extremely complex organizations today dominate a significant portion of the marketplace. It is apparent that, in order to survive, they, too, must develop strategies to address complex issues, and position themselves to meet increasingly intense competition.

Most, if not all, companies are painfully aware of the challenges they will face in the next decade. Companies must develop the overall vision and strategies to not only compete, but to grow and expand in the face of increased competition. Even a company with a well-charted course will encounter roadblocks and operating constraints that will conspire to prevent it from succeeding. In addition to the roadblocks to transition, which can be readily identified, there are conflicting wants of the company that may hinder achievement of its strategic plan.

There are key points to remember.

- A company may face many challenges such as new competition, powerful alliances among competitors, and a shrinking marketplace.
- As a result of mergers and acquisitions, competitors may perform at levels of magnitude greater than traditional and current levels.
- There will be many roadblocks that hinder the company/ organization from responding to the challenges.

- Effective response to the challenge of new competition often requires a dramatic change in a company's processes and practices.

Responding to the Challenges

As we saw briefly in the Introduction, change in the organization is difficult and employees tend to resist change for many reasons. People resist change for two basic reasons: change is perceived to be a threat; and detailed knowledge about the change is frequently not made available. Both of these reasons fuel uncertainties about the future. If the company is critically introspective and honest in assessment of the internal and external conditions affecting strategic planning, it will recognize that there are more motives and incentives for employees to be passive or reactive, than to be active, proactive, and aggressive. Many companies have unintentionally and unwittingly created a passive-reactive "don't fix what isn't broken" mentality. Before it can begin strategic planning, management must respond to these challenges by changing the management culture of the organization. An organizational environment conducive to change is essential for efficient and successful strategic planning.

Some companies favor the business-as-usual approach and see change as a threat to the organizational *status quo*. Once they have become comfortable with the existing lines of responsibility and the process systems within the organization, employees find it difficult to handle change because change brings the threat of something different and unknown. Therefore, change in the organization tends to create fear and resistance in the workforce. The unknown future is what scares employees and causes stressful situations, sometimes impacting negatively on performance and efficiency. Consider the law of physics that says , "For every action there is an equal and opposite reaction." In this case, the action to change causes a reaction within the workforce. Whether that reaction is good or bad depends on those leading the change. Good communication and management of changes affecting the workforce requires leaders and managers to function as dynamic and effective agents of change.

Change can be threatening for many reasons. One of the most common is insecurity. Change, particularly if it is directed from above, often carries a subtle message: things have not been right in this area, and that's why the environment in which you operate must change. That message can be quite threatening.

Change also threatens a person's sense of being in control of his/her environment, particularly when the change is directed from above. In most organizations, an informal organization exists along with the formal one. These are not controlled by managers, but by subordinates who will work vigorously to keep things as they are. When a proposed change in the formal organization also threatens the informal organization, subordinates naturally feel threatened. Since most work gets done through the informal organization, disturbance to it should obviously be held to a minimum.

A feeling of insecurity often exacerbates the threatening aspects of change and any proposed change threatens this equilibrium. Even individuals who were doing good work prior to the change may also feel threatened. If they had advanced as a result of a good relationship with an old manager, the change to a new manager may make them wonder if they will be able to establish a similar relationship with the new one. If an operational change is proposed, such as a change in operations, a change in the direction or focus of marketing efforts, or a change in focus from engineering to services, or vice versa, individuals responsible in each of the affected departments will feel threatened. Job security seems to be the bottom line.

While the need for change may be considered essential to the survival of a business, resistance to change is prevalent. One of the initial causes of feelings of insecurity is a lack of knowledge concerning the need for change. In most cases, employees just have not been made aware of the need to change or the organizational implications of not changing. When change is poorly managed, it can cause irreversible damage, including loss of productivity, morale, and motivation.

Fortunately, effectively managed change can also provide enormous benefits in today's shifting business environment. Well-managed change can also produce remarkable improvements in productivity and morale. While resistance to change can never be completely eliminated, it can be effectively handled when there is a good strategic planning and management process in place.

An essential part of the strategic planning process is in-depth study of management processes already in place. Strategic planners should carefully consider how the organization looks, behaves, and performs today, and how they want it to look, behave, and perform in the future. This is a critical step in becoming a better organization, one that is more productive, focused and participative. Employees must be able to contribute to and share a clear understanding of the organization's vision and mission. Management and employees must work together towards customer satisfaction by delivering quality products at a competitive cost. This will be addressed in greater detail later in this book as we study organizational systems analysis—the strengths, weaknesses, opportunities and threats posed by the inner workings of the organization.

Another term in the strategic planning process that must be defined is *management processes.* Just as a complex luxury automobile is composed of an intricate sequence of processes—design, development, production and maintenance—organizational management is also composed of "processes." For some reason, there is a tendency to be less systematic and disciplined in defining and executing management processes than production processes. However, in today's scramble for business success, the marketplace is seeing more engineering and re-engineering of management systems and processes in order to compete for new business opportunities, and to be more cost effective. Management processes link vision with effective implementation. Effective, high-quality planning can help you successfully respond to the challenge and move toward your vision.

Guiding Principles

Every organization has at its core certain cultures, values, beliefs, and guiding principles. Even in recent years, these characteristics were not common and were certainly not considered in the planning process. However, as quality and productivity programs began to experience difficulties, managers began to talk about the importance of these factors. Guiding principles underlie an organization's values and beliefs; they guide, shape and direct behavior and are the building blocks of corporate culture. Obviously, different organizations will have different guiding principles. Companies in different marketplaces will also have different guiding principles dependent on the product or service they perform and many other factors.

Responsibilities

As we continue to study the planning process, one last consideration needs to be discussed. Who is ultimately responsible for "The Plan"? George A. Steiner lists in his book, *Strategic Planning: What Every*

Manager Must Know, fourteen tasks for which top management is responsible.[5]

1. Deciding what business the company is in and setting objectives for that business
2. Developing concepts, ideas, and plans for achieving those objectives successfully
3. Establishing goals, targets and objectives for the organization
4. Developing a company philosophy, core values, attitudes and guidelines
5. Establishing policies and deciding on plans of action designed to carry them out in accordance with corporate strategy
6. Developing the plan for the organization and deciding on the organization structure
7. Recruiting, staffing, and training of employees to carry out the organization's strategic plan
8. Determining and prescribing how all activities should be carried out
9. Providing the organization's facilities and work spaces to accomplish the business operations
10. Making sure the business has the necessary funding and credit
11. Setting standards by establishing measures of performance that will enable the company to achieve its strategic goals and objectives
12. Ensuring that sufficient resources are made available to conduct strategic planning and management activities
13. Supplying facts and figures to help the workforce follow the strategies, policies and procedures
14. Motivating the workforce to act in accordance with corporate philosophy, policies, procedures, and standards

Steiner correctly points out that planning is prevalent in most of the fourteen tasks and that top management not only has the responsibility, but the conscience to plan for the future of the organization.

The Planning Process

The planning process, as referred to in chapter 1, describes a participative management process involving many members of the organization.

Thompson and Strickland describe four different approaches to strategic planning and eventual development of the Strategic Plan.[6]

1. **The *Chief Architect Approach***
    In this approach a single person shapes most of all of the major strategy for the organization. It is a top-down approach where the strategy is decided at the top and forced down the organization structure.
2. **The *Delegation Approach***
    Here, the top manager delegates big chunks of the strategy-making tasks to trusted subordinates, to lower-level managers in charge of key business units, to a high level task force of knowledgeable and talented people from many parts of the company, to self-directed work teams with authority, or to a team of outside consultants.
3. **The *Collaborative or Team Approach***
    The manager with strategy-making responsibilities enlists the assistance of key peers and subordinates to determine a consensus strategy. This parallels the participative approach discussed in chapter 1.
4. **The *Corporate Intrapreneur***
    Intrapreneurs are simply entrepreneurs who focus on *internal* company operations instead of *external* opportunities. In the intrapreneurial approach, top management encourages individuals and teams to develop and champion proposals for new product lines and new business ventures allowing promising corporate intrapreneurs to use their talents and energies to pursue new strategic initiatives and business opportunities.

Each of these approaches works well in some companies or organizations, but studies suggest that the participative approach has proven the most successful and should be considered when choosing the planning process for your organization. By getting members of the organization involved in the planning process, top management gets support from all levels. This allows for a plan to be filtered up through the organization rather than pushed down. Residual benefits from a participative approach include a more cohesive management team working towards a unified vision and direction; a workforce that accepts the new direction;

and a better-educated middle and lower management team that understands the internal and external factors that impact on the organization.

Ultimate responsibility for leading the tasks of formulating and implementing a strategic plan for the whole organization rests with the top manager, even though many sub-level managers normally have a hand in the process. This planning team is tasked with the objectives of gaining support for the plan from all levels of the organization through recognized participative management procedures. Managers at all levels should be involved in the strategy-making and strategy-implementing process.

One of the primary reasons why middle and lower echelon managers are part of the strategy-making and strategy-implementing teams, is that the more geographically scattered and diversified an organization's operations are, the more unwieldy it becomes for senior executives to craft and implement all the necessary actions and programs. Managers in the corporate headquarters seldom know enough about the situation in every operating unit to direct every move made in the field. More importantly, when the managers who implement the strategy are also the developers of the plan, it is hard for them to shift blame or make excuses if they do not achieve the desired results. Also, since they have participated in developing the strategy they are trying to implement and execute, they are likely to have strong belief in and support for the strategy. When frontline managers have no ownership stake in, or personal commitment to, the strategic plan, there is a tendency to give the plan only minimal support. They may make a few token implementation efforts, and quickly get back to business as usual, knowing that the formal written plan concocted by the planning team carries little weight in shaping their own action agenda and decisions.[7]

A firm's president or CEO characteristically plays the dominant role in the strategic planning process and, in most cases that is needed. It is important, however, that active participation from the rest of the planning team is not minimized simply because the top management shows some reluctance to accept its recommendations. Top management's principal duty often is defined as giving long-term direction to the firm. It is ultimately responsible for the firm's success and, therefore, for the success of its strategy. As described by Mary Coulter, the organization's top manager plays a significant role in the strategic management process as the chief visionary, the chief strategist, and the key decision maker, among other functions.[8] Thompson and Strickland describe the top manager of an organization as the most visible and important strategy maker—

the one responsible to lead in forming, implementing, and executing a strategic plan for the whole organization.[9]

Ultimately, the ideal strategic management team includes decision makers from all company levels, corporate, business, and functional—the chief executive officer, the middle or product managers, and the heads of functional areas. In addition, the team obtains input from company planning staffs, when they exist, and from lower-level managers and supervisors. The latter provide data for strategic decision making and then implement strategies. Because strategic decisions have a tremendous impact on a company and require large commitments of company resources, top managers must give final approval for strategic action.

Notes

1. Arthur A. Thompson, Jr. and A. J. Strickland III, *Strategic Management: Concepts and Cases*, 9th ed., (Chicago: Richard D. Irwin Company, 1996), 2.

2. Peter F. Drucker, *Management: Tasks, Responsibilities, Practices*, (New York: Harper & Row, 1974), 100; cited by Arthur A. Thompson, Jr. and A. J. Strickland III, *Strategic Management: Concepts and Cases* 9th ed., (Chicago: Richard D. Irwin Company, 1996), 34.

3. Arthur A. Thompson, Jr. and A. J. Strickland III, *Strategic Management: Concepts and Cases*, 12th ed., (Boston: McGraw Hill, 2001), 4.

4. Thompson and Strickland, 12th ed., (Boston: McGraw Hill, 2001), 6.

5. George A. Steiner, *Strategic Planning: What Every Manager Must Know*, (New York: Simon & Shuster, 1997), 7–8.

6. Thompson and Strickland, 12th ed., (New York: McGraw Hill, 2001), 23–25.

7. Charles W. L. Hill and Gareth R. Jones, *Strategic Management Theory*, 7th ed., (Boston: Houghton Mifflin, 2007), 127–133.

8. Mary Coulter, *Strategic Management in Action*, 3rd ed., (Upper Saddle River, New Jersey: Prentice Hall, 2005), 13–14.

9. Thompson and Strickland, 12th ed., (New York: McGraw Hill, 2001), 21.

Chapter 3

The Planning Process

It is important to ensure a thorough understanding of planning—what it is and why it is necessary. This chapter serves as a refresher for the student before beginning our study of strategic planning.

In numerous biographical publications of people who are considered successful managers, very few skills seem as important as the ability to plan. It is an expertise actively practiced by successful managers at all levels of the organization. Researchers find that many successful senior level managers believe that the ability to formulate a plan, to identify alternative solutions or courses of action, and decide on the appropriate and cost-effective solution is imperative to good management skills. They also consider the ability and resourcefulness to execute the plan crucial to that expertise. As research would indicate there are many stories of managers who cannot conceive of the plan or derive alternate courses of action, as well as examples of managers who, although they could develop the plan, did not have the ability or resourcefulness to execute it.

To begin, we turn to two well-known experts in management theory: Henri Fayol and Peter Drucker.[1] Written in 1949, the words of Henri Fayol are as true today as they were then. Fayol stresses the importance of planning in the business world and suggests that the plan is a kind of future picture wherein events are outlined and operations are foreseen within a definite period of time. Fayol discusses the importance of a single plan so as not to confuse the organization resulting in uncertainty and disorder. There are five prerequisites that Fayol deems essential for developing a good plan: 1) the art of handling the employees; 2) considerable energy; 3) a measure of moral courage; 4) continuity of tenure; 5) a degree of competence in both specialized and general business experience.

Drucker discusses the importance of long-range planning as a challenge to management science in that planning is a continuous, ongoing process.[2] Drucker indicates that long-range planning cannot be precise since it is almost impossible to forecast events in today's global environment. Drucker presents an interesting perspective for us. He indicates that planning and decision making include the following specifications or elements: objectives, assumptions, expectations, alternative courses of action, decisions, and expected results. Drucker draws one final conclusion from his research: long-range planning is crucial to a business organization and decisions reached through long range planning determine the character and survival of the enterprise.

The consensus of research on the matter indicates that organizational failure (both business and management) can usually be tied to a lack of adequate planning or to non-existent planning. Three underlying principles seem essential for adequate planning to ensure survival of the business.

1. Planning is necessary in any organization for many business purposes, among them development of a strategic plan.
2. Successful managers have the expertise and underlying knowledge and experience to establish and communicate short term and long-range objectives, and then create the necessary policies, procedures, and actions to accomplish them.[3]
3. Long-Range (Strategic) Planning begins with a purpose or a reason for engaging in this action. The resulting process will cause organizational change and managers should be skilled in conflict resolution and change management. The purpose may be to increase profits, become more competitive, reduce costs, and/or expand the business base. In the case of a university, it may be to develop and transmit knowledge; in the case of a hospital, to provide extended healthcare.

Definitions of Planning

Generally, planning (in the context of strategic planning) is considered to be the process of determining organizational goals and how to achieve them. Hill describes strategic planning as involvement of top managers in the context of both current and future competitive environments.[4] Montana indicates that strategic planning involves: 1) choosing a destination, an end result, or an objective; 2) evaluating alternative routes to achieve the intended end result or objective; and 3) deciding on the specific course to reach the chosen destination.[5]

An interesting perspective on planning comes from Marvelle Colby and Selig Alkon in *Introduction to Business*.[6] They contend that planning is the process of establishing the objectives, then setting policies, procedures and a course of action to accomplish these objectives. After setting a purpose, planning goes on to identify objectives and action steps to accomplish it .

By now there should be no doubt that planning is an extremely important element of each manager's job, whether from the corporate view or from the perspective of those who perform day-to-day responsibilities. In today's complex marketplace, the cost of an error because of the old seat-of-the-pants decision-making method can be very high and in some cases catastrophic for the organization. Strategic planning forces managers to sit down and think through issues and alternatives, assess risk, make logical decisions, and attempt to forecast resulting impact on the organization. Through a formal process, managers can assess internal and external forces that affect the organization, develop the vision and mission statements so important to strategic planning, and evaluate every aspect of the organization.

Levels of Planning

In general, there are three somewhat overlapping levels of planning in an organization, with each providing a different level of detail and time framework. In general, planning in an organization can be viewed from three perspectives: Strategic, Long Range, and Operational. As expected, just as different organizations embody different planning different authors define the levels of planning somewhat differently. But one thing is clear: planning is every manager's job. Planning philosophies or processes may be similar or slightly different but researchers agree that planning is an important function in every organization and must be practiced by all levels of managers in the organization structure.

Strategic Planning

Strategic Planning differs from planning in general only in the length of time that the plan considers and the complexity of the plan in terms of what part of the organization is addressed. In other words, if the plan addresses only one aspect of the organization such as its financial, marketing, engineering, production, or safety, it is not truly the organization's *strategic plan*, which would encompass all of these.

Strategic planning is a complex process that requires extensive resources, and considers all aspects of the organization including everything that comes into it and that goes out of it. Strategic planning has a long time-frame and looks at the future in terms of the entire organization's vision and mission. Strategic plans should be differentiated from other types of plans within the organization.

Distinct Characteristics of Strategic Planning[7]

TIME FRAME: Usually a relatively long period, perhaps five years, or even longer

BASIC QUESTIONS: What business are we in? What is our marketplace? Should we broaden or shrink our business? What is our road map for success?

PROCESS: It probably involves several top executives—perhaps members of the board of directors—and heavy use of staff personnel in participative management procedures involving all employees.

COMPLEXITY: It deals with many variables, because both the external environment and the internal environment must be assessed and strengths, weaknesses, and opportunities reviewed.

DEGREE OF STRUCTURE: Strategic Planning tends to be viewed differently by each organization depending on the culture, philosophy, and personnel within the organization.

Long-range Planning

In our context, long-range planning has a time frame shorter than strategic planning. It addresses some of the components of the strategic plan, and may include many organizational areas such as safety, security, marketing, finance, business strategy, and so on. Long-range plans in the organization should be complementary to the overall strategic plan. They can be considered to be implementation plans at subordinate levels within the organization and may include portions of the strategic plan as appropriate, identifying market conditions, financial objectives, and the resources necessary to complete that particular plan. All long-range planning is done within the framework of the strategic plan. This intermediate level of planning can be viewed as the bridge between strategic planning and day-to-day operational planning. Like strategic planning, long-range planning has its own characteristics.[8]

> TIME FRAME: Shorter than strategic planning, usually 1-5 years.
> BASIC QUESTIONS: What are the major components of our business? Are there specific areas of concentration during this time frame?
> PROCESS: Same as strategic planning
> COMPLEXITY: Although complex, long-range planning addresses fewer variables since the vision and mission have already been stated in the strategic plan. A variety of data sources such as financial returns, market conditions, and organizational resources, are considered. External data are reviewed.

Operational Planning

Operational planning has an even shorter time frame than long-range planning. It is day-to-day planning of specific timetables, tasks, and measurable targets. It involves managers in each unit who will be responsible for achieving the plan targets.

Some Popular Planning Tools

Many tools and techniques exist to assist managers in the planning process. The first basic tool is the organization's policy and procedures manual. It is here that policies can be found which dictate precisely what may and what may not be done within the organization. Specific policies would indicate what organization members should or should not do, whereas general policies or non-specific policies furnish broad guidelines for making decisions and taking action. Examples of specific policies: All employees must begin work by 9:00 AM; there is no smoking in the building under any conditions; sexual misconduct will not be tolerated. Examples of general policies (non-specific) policies: The company policy is to send flowers to funerals of immediate family members of employees; the company will reimburse employees for college education courses, providing a B average is maintained.

A second planning tool is the organization's budget. A budget is a financial plan that covers a specific period. It details how funds will be obtained (cash in) and how funds will be allocated or expensed (cash out). Budgets should reflect each source of cash in as well as each item of expense or cash out. In addition, the budget should include a description of how money will be spent as well as limits on how much is to be spent for each expense item. Budgets are established as a planning tool so that employees know how to operate on a daily basis for the duration of the budget.

Planning Models

There are three well known planning models: the Backwards Planning, the PERT, and the Gantt.

Backwards Planning

The backwards planning method is a simple planning technique developed and used extensively by the military. The method starts with the desired final result or objective of the plan and then develops all the sequential actions, starting with the final objective and working backwards identifying each required prior action and the resources needed. As each preceding task is identified, the time and resources required to achieve it are estimated. Determining the starting date is then simple, as it merely requires adding the times required for each task and backing up from the desired completion date.

Program Evaluation, and Review Technique (PERT) Planning

The PERT system is sometimes called "Bubble Charts" because of its recording of tasks inside bubble-like circles which are interrelated and connected by arrows to other bubbles. PERT was developed in the late 1950s to address the complexities of the Polaris missile program. That program required many highly sophisticated and technically complex engineering and manufacturing activities to occur at the proper time and in the proper sequence in order to meet cost and schedule requirements. PERT was created to assist in the sequential planning and controlling of a series of interrelated events.

PERT uses a formalized graphical approach. Conceptually it is a continuation of the backwards planning method, so if you understand the backwards planning method, the wisdom inherent in the PERT will be readily apparent. It goes several steps beyond the backwards method by depicting the time phasing (time to complete each action item) and the logical inter-relationships among the tasks. Use of the PERT also permits the total time required to complete the project to be readily discerned. It also shows which parts of the project are essential to project success—the "critical path." The critical path is also defined as the inter-related tasks that require the most time to complete. Completion of each task allows progression to the next task and thereby indicates the minimum completion time.

The PERT shows how each task leads to the next and depicts the logical relationship of one task to another. When applied properly, the PERT is very useful for ensuring that all required tasks have been identified.

Gantt Planning

In the Gantt planning method, charts are used to show the time phasing and scheduling of events necessary to reach an objective. The Gantt chart displays tasks in the form of an input triangle with a bar or line representing continuing action. The conclusion of the action is represented by an inverse triangle.

Several problems limit the effectiveness of Gantt charts as planning tools. One of the most immediate is that there is nothing built into a Gantt chart that assures completion of one task will logically allow initiation of the next, or that all the necessary tasks have been identified. For that reason, a Gantt chart, used alone, is a poor management review tool, even though it is widely used for that purpose. Gantt charts are best used as a management tool *after* a plan has been developed with the PERT method. Once all the tasks have been identified, they can be placed into a Gantt chart. Then the Gantt chart can be used to track progress by moving a vertical line to represent the current time. All tasks to the left of this time line should be complete; if they are not, they are behind schedule.

Planning Responsibilities

Top-level managers have the ability to influence many operational procedures in an organization. The amount of control or influence within a manager's comfort zone will dictate how much control he or she will relinquish to the planning team. Some top managers are very dictatorial and will relinquish very little control or authority to the planning team; other managers require less control and will relinquish more authority to team. Managers' personal style, the amount of control and influence they exert, and how they define appropriate and effective management and leadership behavior, will vary from situation to situation. There is ample proof that management and leadership have become more complex and require a wider range of behaviors. Simply put, managers/ leaders can exert widely varying amounts of control and influence over company operations, including development of the Strategic Plan. The degree of influence or control is typically based on the personality of each manager/leader. For example autocratic control is not always bad, just as participative management is not always good for the organization. The particular style of management is often dependent on where the organization is in its life cycle. A good example can be found by reading two contrasting books: *Jack: Straight from the Gut*, by Jack Welch, former CEO of General Electric, and *Mean Business* . . . (his title not mine) by "Chainsaw Al" Dunlap, former CEO at Sunbeam and other companies .These books present polar opposites in top-levels management styles.[9]

The effectiveness of a particular management and leadership style, especially in the development of the strategic plan, depends on a variety of factors: the need for control of what goes on in the organization; the need for acceptance; the need for quality; the availability of time; and the developmental level of the followers (employees). There is much research on this subject and this document will not delve into the factors driving management and leadership control. Suffice it to say that the amount of control and influence that top management exercises during development of the strategic plan depends largely on how comfortable top managers are with giving subordinate managers a voice in the planning process.

Summary

Thorough in-depth strategic planning and management is a step-by-step process. The first step is to develop a list of objectives that define how the organization plans to achieve its mission. These objectives can be expressed in statements such as, "This company plans to continue providing electronic products and services to the automotive industry," or, "Our company plans to continue supplying quality computers to selected industries." Objectives are generally expressed in specific terms and are tied to a definite time frame. Even though a business has a single purpose and a single mission, it will usually have multiple objectives. Objectives usually include goals stated in measurable steps that provide guidelines for reaching those objectives. Specific sales revenues, growth rates, and profits are examples of some of the more common objectives. Broad objectives must be converted to specific actions, usually stated in terms of an action plan. An action plan may be classified as either strategic or tactical.

A strategic plan, then, becomes the formal document that describes the vision, mission, objectives, and actions of a company over a long-term period—frequently five to ten years. In other words, it describes the company's long-term strategy. Most research indicates that strategic plans prepared by a planning team comprised of managers from all levels of the company, led by the top level of management, and approved by the company board of directors, are most influential and successful. Full discussion of these plans is presented in later chapters.

It is essential for the survival of an organization that its managers—at all levels—develop expert planning skills. Early in development of a strategic plan, managers might well assume that their firm's competitors have previously engaged in strategic planning and, consequently, already have a competitive edge. The competition may already be focused on achieving their vision, and already be moving towards accomplishing strategic goals, and practicing shared management, thus significantly improving their productivity. There is a lot to do to catch up; the company must keep pace with its competition or be left in the dust. Astute managers know that in business, as well as in other ventures, the old saying rings true: "Lead, follow, or get out of the way."

From all the reasons enumerated here, top management will recognize the need to institute a formal strategic planning process within the organization.

Finally, in order that students see the beginning-to-end sequence of actions necessary to develop the organization's strategic plan, a step-by-step list is presented.

1.   The organization establishes a planning team and with a team leader, all drawn from managers and selected employees at each level of the organization.
2.   The leader of the organization creates and communicates the company's vision and reinforces the company's mission with broad statements about its purpose, philosophy, and goals.
3.   The planning team conducts a formal, in-depth analysis of company processes—an analysis that reflects the company's internal and external capabilities and conditions, including the competition and the marketplace.
4.   In conjunction with the company leadership, the planning team establishes an extensive list of long-range strategic goals and mid-to-short-term tactical objectives.
5.   The planning team, in conjunction with the company leadership, analyzes the organization's options by matching its resources with the external environment.
6.   Based on that analysis, the planning team—in conjunction with the company leadership—identifies the most desirable options by evaluating each option in light of the company's vision and mission and the available resources.
7.   The planning team then sets forth strategic goals that can be accomplished with the resources available, that will achieve the most desirable options, and that will accomplish the vision.
8.   Based on the strategic goals identified in step 7, the planning team develops one- and two-year tactical objectives and short-term strategies that serve to help reach each strategic goal.
9.   In conjunction with top management, and after consideration of the operational environment, the planning team creates process action teams that are assigned specific tactical objectives to be accomplished within the approved time frame.
10. Following implementation of tactical objectives and accomplishment of strategic goals, top leadership of the company evaluates the success of the strategic process in terms of measureable goals and objectives.

11. Strategic planning becomes a way of life for an organization intent on overcoming the competition and becoming even more successful.

Notes

1. Cited by Michael T. Matteson and John M. Ivancevich, eds., *Management and Organizational Behavior Classics,* 7th ed., (Boston: Irwin McGraw Hill, 1999), 69-76. Henri Fayol, *General and Industrial Management*, (London: Sir Isaac Pitman and Sons, Ltd., 1949), 43-52.

2. Matteson and Ivancevich, 77-89; and Peter F. Drucker, "Long Range Planning: a Challenge to Management Science," *Management Science*, v 5, n 3, 1959, 238-49.

3. Patrick J. Montana and Bruce H. Charnov, *Management*, 3rd ed., (New York: Barron's Educational Series, 1993), 117.

4. Charles W. L. Hill and Gareth R. Jones, *Strategic Management Theory*, 7th ed., (Boston: Houghton Mifflin Company, 2007), 25.

5. Montana and Charnov, 118.

6. Marvelle S. Colby and Selig Alkon, *Introduction to Business*, (New York: Harper Collins Publishers, 1991), 75-77.

7. The information reflected in this table/figure represents data collected and synopsized by Dr. Bertocci from many sources to fit into this format. The original sources of the data were Thompson and Strickland, eds., *Strategic Management*, 9th and 12th editions; Mary Coulter, *Strategic Management in Action*, 3rd edition; and Charles W. L. Hill and Gareth R. Jones, *Strategic Management Theory*, 7th ed.

8. Ibid. The information reflected in this table/figure represents data that was collected and synopsized by Dr. Bertocci from many sources to fit into this format. The original source of the data primarily included material from the two books by Thompson and Strickland, Strategic Management 9th and 12th edition, the book by Mary Coulter, Strategic Management in Action, 3rd edition, and the book by Charles W.L. Hill and Gareth R. Jones, Strategic Management Theory, 7th ed.

9. Jack Welch and John A. Byrne, *Straight from the Gut*, (New York: Warner Business Books, 2001); and "Chainsaw Al" Dunlap with Bob Andelman, *Mean Business: How I Save Bad Companies and Make Good Companies Great,*(New York: Simon and Schuster/Fireside, 1997).

Chapter 4

The Strategic Planning Process

As we discussed in Chapter 3, planning in a successful organization should be done throughout all operational levels. Thorough and complete planning—considering all alternatives and examining all of the factors impacting the organization—requires time and effort on the part of the planning committee. Strategic planning demands extensive data gathering and data analysis, both of which are time-consuming functions.

Hill and Jones have an interesting perspective on the levels of strategic planning within an organization.[1] They indicate that a company is a collection of functions or departments that work together to provide products and/or services to the marketplace, and that there are three main levels of planning: corporate, business and functional. Each should have a separate operational plan but the overriding strategic plan should incorporate each level. For a slightly different view, Mary Coulter provides an interesting perspective on strategic planning and management.[2] She describes strategic planning and management as the ability to anticipate, envision, maintain flexibility, think strategically, and initiate changes that will create a viable and valuable future for the organization. Further she indicates that there are six key dimensions identified with strategic leadership: determining the vision or purpose; exploiting and maintaining core capabilities; developing human capital; creating and sustaining strong organizational culture; emphasizing ethical decisions and practices; and establishing appropriately balanced controls.

Strategic Planning Approaches

As we saw earlier, Thompson and Strickland describe four different strategic planning approaches.

1. The Chief Architect Approach
2. The Delegation Approach
3. The Collaborative or Team Approach
4. The Corporate Intrapreneur Approach[3]

Each of the four approaches has merit, each has strengths and weaknesses, and each is workable in the right situation. The process described in this book is a modification of their Collaborative or Team Approach and is thought to be one of the most effective approaches for most businesses. We have labeled it the *participative approach.*

In the participative approach, top-level management appoints a planning committee and a facilitator to conduct the actual planning sessions. In this approach, top management is a member of the planning team but not the leader of the planning effort, whereas in the Thompson and Strickland collaborative approach, top management is not a member of the planning team. The intent of the participative approach is to create an environment whereby input to the plan is solicited from all levels of the organization. Representatives of different factions of the work force are expected to bring input to the planning meetings from those they represent. Some junior members of the work force who have the ability to think creatively should be included in the planning team. Experienced members of the workforce who have the ability "to tell it like it is" should also be included. Care must be taken to include all levels of management in the planning process in order to encourage support across the entire organization. The participative approach is intended to give people a stake in creating the strategic plan so that when called upon to implement it, they bring prior knowledge and acceptance. Since they were part of the team that created it, the plan became theirs. In this approach, top management helps the team catch the vision and then formulate the mission statement. It also provides coordination, staff resources, and support for the planning process.

Planning Considerations

Developing a strategic plan for any organization can be a significant drain on precious resources. Consider the time, the facilities used during the planning process, and the amount of funding dedicated to the planning team, as well as to the implementation team. It is essential that the chief executive of the organization support development of the strategic plan. He or she must endorse the planning process, foster it, and communicate the importance of the strategic plan to the well-being of the company. The chief executive contributes to this by providing resources and facilities for the planning team, and by permitting the planning process to take place during normal working hours. In cases when the planning process takes place after hours, the planning team is compensated for that extra time.

The participative approach to strategic planning, as set forth in this book, is a proven method of identifying where the company is compared to its competition, where the company wants to be, and how the company is going to get there. This planning process establishes specific actions, priorities, responsibilities, required resources, and milestones against which to measure attainment of the strategic goals. The strategic planning process emphasizes that the key to improvement lies with the excellent performance of the employees, as well as with management's training and expertise, as well as its commitment to complete the planning process and then to implement the plan. The participative approach has been implemented successfully in a number of public and private organizations. But since no organization is exactly like any other, there is no single planning process best suited for every organization. Any planning process must be tailored to and modified for each organization.

It has been proven that proper execution of this process will result in a thorough and well-supported plan. The process is highly participative and ensures that the plan itself will be responsive to the various needs of the organization; it is designed to be completed in several sessions including a top management session, as well as an orientation session for all employees. This process for strategic planning is a formal, systematic approach to improving organizational performance as it emphasizes existing customer-supplier relationships and features a top-down, structured, participative, and measurement-oriented approach to planning for system improvements. The process emphasizes long-term leadership commitment and top-down implementation; critical customer satisfaction;

commitment to teamwork and participation at all levels; prevention of problems rather than reaction to them; commitment to continuous process improvement; management by fact, not opinion; both job-related training and training in continuous process improvement; and recognizing employee success at all levels.

The participative planning process incorporates certain TQM principles, recognizing that the process by which you plan is almost as important as the plan you produce. It employs a very detailed organizational self-analysis as its initial starting point. For many organizations, the plan (the product) becomes the primary focus, when the introspective process and analysis of the organization's vision, mission, input and output should be the primary focus; those functions are more beneficial in the long term. If the objective is simply to develop a plan without much in-depth consideration of tradeoffs between acceptance, timeliness, quality, and ultimate effective implementation, then the return on the assets invested in the process will be small. Research has shown that successful managers follow a rather formal, orderly approach, characterized by careful and structured planning; they understand that improving the system is an evolutionary procedure. Successful managers see planning as a production process somewhat similar to the ones that produce goods or services. Research reveals several key principles to consider as part of the planning process. Some of these are simply a slight modification of the Fourteen Principles of Management set forth by Dr. W. Edwards Deming.[4]

- The process by which you plan is as important as the plan itself.
- Those who must implement the plan should be involved in the development of the plan.
- Top management support and involvement is a precondition for success.
- A thorough analysis of the internal and external factors involving the organization is essential to success.
- A vision of where the company is, where it wants to go, and how it is going to get there, is an essential part of the planning process. It begins with a vision of the future that leads to actions that can be initiated "Monday morning."
- The mission statement must convey what the company does and what customer base it supports.

- The plan is not finished until its implementation is completed.
- The planning process should be a group-oriented effort, designed to tap the wisdom of the entire team.
- The planning process should be structured, but not rigidly formal.

Planning Methodology

The participative approach employed in this planning process has been designed to incorporate considerations of time availability, need for acceptance, need for quality, as well as willingness and ability of the participants. It is based upon the assumption that the ultimate desired outcomes of strategic planning are clear direction for the company, improved competitiveness in the marketplace, a more cohesive workforce, and improved performance.

This strategic planning methodology, a five-step process for developing a long-range plan, is designed to be completed by a carefully selected planning team. It is essentially a set of closely interrelated steps. Each step is made up of sub-steps that are used to accomplish its objective. This planning methodology, then, becomes a component of a larger planning, programming, and budgeting system within the organization.

It is important that the strategic plan is clearly communicated and reasonably easy to buy into. So how do we get from conceptually agreeing to development of a strategic plan to actually developing the plan—creating a document that will excite the work force, communicate clearly to customers and suppliers what we do and what our goals and expectations are? The next sections of this book focus on a detailed description of just such a tried and tested planning process. It has been designed and engineered to overcome many of the problems with planning processes encountered in the past. It is a structured process, with specific techniques that enable your organization to initiate and carry out strategic planning.

Planning Paradigms

Before beginning the discussion of the specific planning process, we point out some traditional paradigms that still come to mind when students think about strategic planning. The list below provides only a sample of such misconceptions about strategic planning.

- Only top management makes plans, so there is no need for anyone lower to consider strategic planning.
- There are planners and there are doers.
- To be efficient, planning should be done in a non-participative fashion. The "boss" knows what we need and how we should be organized. He has been successful in running this company so why should we change?
- Planning is an art only and no formal process needs to be considered.
- Since planning is so painful and difficult, it must be done at an expensive resort.
- The plan is more important than the process of developing the plan.
- There is one best way to plan.
- There isn't a structured way to plan.
- You can't plan with more than three to five people in the room; involving all managers and employees in the planning process would be inefficient and ineffective.
- People at the top think best; that's why they're at the top.
- We do too much planning already; our existing planning process isn't perfect but it works. You only need to do planning for capital, facilities, staffing, and marketing; anything else is redundant.
- Planning is something you do when you don't have anything else to do or when someone tells you to do it.

These and other misconceptions, even if held by only one member of the planning team, can negatively impact the planning process and may impede progress in performance improvement for the competitive organization of the future. *These perceptions must be replaced; success of the organization is at stake.*

Core Values

Its core values are the heart of every organization. Those listed below are important considerations for almost every organization:

1. What the company stands for—its mission and vision
2. What the company places much value on
3. How the company treats its employees
4. How the company treats its customers
5. What the company delivers in terms of product quality
6. What the company's expectations are

There are some examples typical of the planning principles and core values normally established by top management to be considered and embraced by the planning team.

- Quality is vital to our business, and requires a commitment to continuous improvement on the part of all personnel.
- A quality- and productivity-oriented business base is central to our maintaining a superior level of growth and expansion.
- Sustained emphasis on and concern for both high quality and productivity must be integral to every daily activity.
- Quality improvement is a key to productivity improvement and must be pursued with all the resources necessary to produce tangible results.
- The best available technology—one of our greatest assets—must be used wherever possible for continuous improvement in the quality of equipment and services.
- From the very beginning, emphasis must be on designing and building quality into both the process and the product.
- High quality must be embraced as a key element of competition.
- Managers and employees at all levels must take responsibility for the quality of their efforts.
- Competent, dedicated employees make the greatest contributions to quality and productivity. They must be recognized and rewarded accordingly.
- Quality concepts must be instilled throughout the organization through proper training at every level.
- Principles of quality improvement must involve all personnel and products.

The Step-by-Step Planning Process

Step One

As in any journey, the first step begins the process. Before writing the plan, before selection of a planning team, before conducting the first planning session, the very first step is the decision by top management to support the strategic planning process with the time and resources necessary for the complete the life cycle of the strategic plan—from beginning to implementation. Once the decision is made to actually begin such a planning process, top management selects a strategic planning leader—someone who will guide the planning effort. There are several methods of selecting such a leader. Often someone in the company's organization already holds the position responsible for planning. But if no such position exists, the task can be given either to a qualified planning consultant or a key individual in the company who has shown an interest in planning, is endorsed by top management and is senior enough to have in-depth understanding of company processes and functions.

Step Two

In step two, the designated strategic planner meets with top management of the organization. This meeting sets the stage for the actual planning sessions and serves to clarify expected outcomes from formal strategic planning. An initial design (ID) session with top management is scheduled to develop the agenda for the planning meetings. These meetings must be conducted within the framework of the organization and take into account the time, facilities and resources available. This usually requires involvement of top management of the organization. The ID session could take four to eight hours—longer depending on the complexity of the organization. Typically the only participants in these initial design sessions should be members of the planning team and a few representatives from top management.

In a design session, the objective is not to develop the plan, but to design the agenda for the planning sessions. Part of the initial design session is to establish the ground rules for the planning sessions and to determine the outcomes desired for each. One purpose of the first planning session is to review the vision and suggest any changes needed to clarify or expand it. The desired outcome for step two is to develop "ownership" of the agenda by top management. Their desires—and perhaps even their hidden agendas—must be brought to the surface at the planning session if other participants are to be assured of top management's genuine support and involvement.

Step Three

As planning moves forward, the next step is to identify and select a planning team. It should be made of a group of people from within the organization who have varied backgrounds and perspectives. It is essential that top management be included as well as representatives of the middle levels of management, together with some representation from the workforce at lower levels. Often junior-level people are selected to be on the planning term for their skills in technology as well as their fresh perspective, while senior level people are often included because of their extensive experience and long history with the company. The group must be large enough and representative enough to ensure both inter-group and extra-group consensus. A critical issue is whether the resulting plan will be accepted, based upon non-participants' perception of the quality of people who generated it. On the other hand, the group must be small enough to ensure that the sessions can be reasonably efficient. A successful planning team includes individuals who are able both to avoid bias and to ensure that each faction of the company gets equal time. It should also include a planning facilitator who is not part of the organization.

In my experience, representatives on the planning team must have the ability to voice their opinions in planning sessions, be able to formulate and present productive ideas, not be intimidated by upper management in presenting their ideas, and be willing and able to interface with the group they are representing in order to gather ideas and form a consensus for presentation at the planning sessions. Keep in mind that one of the results of the planning process is to get a majority of the workforce to accept and embrace the plan as theirs—in effect, to support the planners' vision, goals, and objectives as if they were their own.

Step Four

Next comes the actual planning sessions in which formal analysis and planning occur. As mentioned earlier, the sessions will normally take place in an off-site location, using as many days as practical, considering the size and complexity of the company. An off-site location is frequently selected so participants will be able to fully dedicate themselves to the task and not be distracted by telephone calls, customers, and other demands of routine business. Specific tasks to be accomplished at this step are discussed in later chapters. However, it is at this step that organizational analysis and the setting of goals and objectives takes place.

Step Five

The final step is to begin implementation of the strategic goals and tactical objectives developed during the planning sessions. As part of this effort, the planning team will convert the goals and objectives into action items and select process action teams to carry out specific actions.

Each of these steps will also be discussed in detail in later chapters.

Notes

1. Charles W. L. Hill and Gareth R. Jones, *Strategic Management Theory*, 7th ed., (New York: Houghton Mifflin Company, 2007), 9.
2. Mary Coulter, *Strategic Management in Action*, 3d ed. (Upper Saddle River, NJ: Pearson Education, 2005).
3. Thompson and Strickland, *Strategic Management: Concepts and Cases*, 12th ed., (New York: McGraw Hill Companies, 2001), 23-25.
4. Mary Walton, *The Deming Management Method*. (New York: Putnam Publishing Group, 1986).

Chapter 5

Organizational Systems Analysis: Vision and Mission

The planning team has been selected and the initial design session with top management has been completed. The stage is now set: the preliminaries are finished and development of the strategic plan can begin. We are now ready to examine the factors related to its development.

Methods of Analysis

There are actually two formal processes to examine the company's operations. One is the OSA (Organization Systems Analysis) and the other is imbedded in the more-familiar SWOT (Strengths, Weaknesses, Opportunities and Threats) process. The main difference between the two is that the OSA tends to be a much deeper, more thorough analysis of all the components using a systematic approach, whereas SWOT tends to only look at the components of the process itself.

The first method (OSA) is a major planning process that examines all the internal and external factors that will impact the strategic plan. It is a formal procedure used to examine each and every system and process within the company as a prelude to creating the strategic plan. The OSA is a tool used by planners to accurately and thoroughly understand exactly where they are. It features an in-depth and very detailed analysis of the company's operation and processes. The OSA is the basis for choosing a strategy which matches organizational resources, competencies, and competitive capabilities. It is the most important part of the planning process—absolutely essential before strategic goals and objectives are developed. There are several intricate processes within the company that must be examined in depth. Strategic planners need to understand them thoroughly in order to shape a realistic strategy.

- What is really going on inside the company? This includes both formal and informal lines of communication, personnel issues, operational issues, and stockholder issues.
- What is coming into the company in terms of supplies and products, as well as any requirements—in terms of budgets, policies, and procedures,—that are being imposed upon the firm by its parent organization?
- What is going out from the company—products, services, documents, letters, and so on?
- What do suppliers provide and when do problems with deadlines and similar issues occur?
- How are employees organized, is the chain of command working, and is the organization chart accurate?
- What are the factors to be considered such as median age of the workforce, unions within the company, employment contracts and other human resources factors?
- What is processed/produced within the company?
- What functions are outsourced to subcontractors?
- What external factors affect the organization, e.g., severe weather, transport strikes, and shipping resources?
- Who are the customers, what are their requirements, and what changes can be expected in those requirements?
- What is the competitive marketplace and what is the competition doing?
- What is preventing the company from achieving its present strategic goals?
- What does the company do (good and bad) and how is it done?

Many strategy makers endorse a more popular process called the Strengths, Weaknesses, Opportunities, Threats (SWOT) concept. This very popular process is used by many organizations. However, I believe the Organizational System Analysis (OSA) is better suited for use in today's business world because it uses a scientific, more structured process to examine essentially the same areas that SWOT addresses. Each method is simply a tool for looking at all the factors as part of the planning process. In either case, the purpose is to examine in depth the internal and external functions, processes and factors that affect who the company is, what it does, and how it does it.

Components of Organization Systems Analysis

Organization Systems Analysis examines eight areas in the development of a Strategic Plan.

- The Vision Statement—an articulated "picture" of what the organization can be—the direction for the company to follow
- The Mission Statement—an enduring statement of the purpose of the organization that states what the company does or what the company makes and for whom
- The Input Analysis—a formal systematic assessment of everything that comes into the organization including customer requirements, supplier-provided products used to complete the organization's own product or services, budgets or policies imposed by a parent company, personnel issues and any other external factors that affect the organization
- The Output Analysis—a formal assessment of products, services, documents, analyses—everything that goes out from the company
- Roadblocks—identification and assessment of impediments that keep the organization from accomplishing its mission and vision
- The Internal Strategic Analysis—identification and assessment of internal strengths such as seniority and expertise of the workforce, any technological advantages the company has over the competition, or any other unique factor that distinguishes the organization from the competition
- The External Strategic Analysis—identifies and assesses such external opportunities as anticipated new requirements from customers, emerging business opportunities, potential new markets and product lines, as well as anticipated changes in the makeup of the workforce
- The Strategic Planning Assumptions—hypotheses about future events that are likely to impact the organization—such

what if questions as how might a union strike, bankruptcy of
our suppliers, or sudden retirement of many of our experienced workers impact our future

Certainly, this is not an exhaustive list, and organizations may and
should tailor it to fit their needs. An organization may not fully examine
each area during the first cycle. Trade-offs must be made between time
constraints and the amount of information that is examined or analyzed.

There are several well-known techniques for conducting an in-depth
analysis of a company's operation. Any of these can be used as long as
they examine each element of the operation and arrive at an in-depth
understanding of the process, objective, and result of that function. A
structured internal and external analysis is intended to thoroughly examine aspects of the organization before beginning development of the plan
itself.

The Vision Statement

The first, and probably the most important element in the organization
systems analysis is the vision. The vision of the organization's leader
binds everyone in the company together. It tells both employees and
customers what the company is trying to do and what it wants to become.
The vision enables everyone in the company to know and understand
management's overriding plan for the organization.

Developing a carefully constructed vision statement pushes managers to consider what the company's business character is, and to develop
a clear picture of where the company needs to head in the next five to ten
years. The vision statement clarifies who the company is, what it does,
and where it is headed. It charts a course for the organization to take and
helps establish a strong organizational identity. The vision represents
what your organization must become in order to compete and survive in
the future; it reflects the grand strategy that guides the company's evolution. A well-conceived strategic vision prepares a company for the future, establishes long-term direction, and indicates the company's intent
to embrace a particular business position.

Mary Coulter describes the vision as, "a broad comprehensive picture of what a leader wants the organization to become. It is a statement
of what the organization stands for, what it believes in, and why it exists."[1] Hill and Jones describe the vision as a desired future state, articu-

lating what the company would like to achieve.[2] Thompson and Strickland talk about the vision as a statement that conveys a larger sense of purpose so that employees see themselves as building a cathedral rather than laying stones. Further they indicate that a strategic vision creates enthusiasm for the course management has charted, engages members of the organization, and illuminates the direction in which the organization is headed.[3]

The leader with a vision provides an organization with an all-important bridge from the present to the future. A vision cannot be established by edict or coercion; it is more an act of persuasion, of creating an enthusiastic and dedicated commitment towards the future. The effective vision is right for the times, right for the organization, and most important of all, right for the people working toward it. By focusing attention on a vision, the leader operates on the emotional and spiritual resources of the organization—its values, commitment, and aspirations.

My research found that there are many perceptions of what the strategic vision should be. Some authors include the vision statement as part of the mission statement. Others discount the importance of a vision statement. However, I think there is consensus that the strategic vision always refers, first, to a future condition of the organization—a state that does not presently exist, but that the organization is trying attain. Second, the strategic vision "draws" rather than "pushes" an organization into the future by getting the workforce to share in the excitement of knowing where they are going and how they are going to get there. A shared vision is a powerful, energizing force in any organization; it breeds alignment in the common quest for an improved future state. The third power of a vision is its ability to produce in individuals commitment to a common view of success for the organization. Thompson and Strickland assert, "There's no escaping the need for a strategic vision."[4] Casting a strategic vision and stating it clearly is the responsibility of an organization's top management. Those leaders must have a firm grasp of where the company is and where it has to go, and then communicate that vision to both employees and customers. It is the creation of a compelling vision that separates successful leaders or managers from unsuccessful ones. The successful leader/manager must also know how to convert the strategic vision into reality through the strategic planning process. There are several key points to remember in creating the strategic vision.

- The vision statement conceptually suggests a systematic "grand strategy" that will guide the organization's evolution from the present to the future.
- By focusing attention on a vision, top management takes advantage of the emotional and spiritual resources of the organization—its values, commitment, and aspirations—and of the physical resources of the organization—its capital, human skills, raw material, and technology.
- With a vision, top management provides the all-important bridge from the present to the future of the organization.
- A vision projects the view of a realistic, credible, attractive future for the organization, a condition better in some important ways than what now exists.
- The vision grabs and pulls people toward it and provides a unified purpose.
- A vision always refers to a future state, a condition that does not presently exist.
- The vision animates, inspires, and transforms purpose into action.
- The vision should be projected in time and space beyond the boundaries of short-term planning activities.

The term, "organization of the future," represents a vision of what the organization must become in order to compete and survive. It is a grand concept that must portray the desired evolution from the present to the future. This is what shapes a strategic plan. Collectively, researchers find that effective leaders pay attention to the challenges posed by the competition, evaluate the changing global marketplace, set a new direction for the company to follow, and convey that vision to the workforce.

Guiding Principles/Core Values

Guiding principles (core values) are the second element in Organization Systems Analysis. These are the rules, policies, business models, and in-place procedures that guide the company in its daily operations. Policies that mirror the Golden Rule would be appropriate for this element. Considerations also include the ethics that guide the company, its compliance with environmental regulations, how the company acts during times of strife, how it treats both customers and employees, what employees can and cannot do, as well as other major declarations that inform employees and customers what the company considers ethical performance and standards for its daily operations. At this point in plan development, the planning team identifies those guiding principles or core values that directly impact development of the strategic plan.

The Mission Statement

The third element in the Organizational Systems Analysis is creation of a mission statement that describes what the organization does by defining the scope of the company's business. A well-worded mission statement defines what business the company is in. It expresses the very reason for the organization's existence. For example, the mission of General Motors is to produce cars—it is what defines the company. Can you imagine General Motors changing its mission from producing cars to making something else? Or Dell? Or Microsoft? A mission statement should have a sense of permanence. It should serve as a motivational force for employees, as well as provide a guide to decision making. It provides a sense of focus and a core purpose that shape its choice of strategies.

This does not imply that mission statements are never changed. But this would happen only in rare circumstances. Redefining the company mission may be necessary due to its deliberate expansion or as a response to competitive pressures that require it to alter its product, market, or technology. When a revised mission statement is formulated, it should contain the same components as the original and should clearly state the basic type of product or service then to be offered, the primary markets or customer groups to be served, the technology to be used in production or delivery, the firm's fundamental concern for survival through growth and profitability, the firm's managerial philosophy, the public image the firm seeks, and the image of the firm held by those within it.

Mary Coulter portrays the mission statement as a description of what specific organizational units do and what they hope to accomplish in alignment with the organizational vision.[5] Hill and Jones go a bit further by indicating that a mission statement has four main components: a statement of the reason for existence of the company; a statement of some desired future state; a statement of the key values that the organization is committed to; and a statement of its major goals.[6] Though both definitions address a company's mission statement, the one proposed by Hill and Jones is more complex.

Once an organization establishes its purpose, it communicates that purpose in its mission statement. Its mission is what a company does—its reason for existing. The purpose of any commercial business is to make a profit; its m ission—the way it seeks to achieve that purpose—is to manufacture products or provide services. Within a particular industry other firms may adopt variations of the same mission. In the automotive industry General Motors, Ford, Toyota, Honda, Nissan, and others each manufacture automobiles but in different ways and with different goals and objectives. Ferrari or Maserati, for example, may have as its mission "to manufacture high-performance sports cars," but its *purpose* is still to make a profit.

A major challenge in developing a mission statement is recognizing when emerging opportunities and threats make it desirable to revise the organization's long-term direction. In order to arrive at a new mission statement, management has to understand the total business enterprise and its rapidly-changing internal and external environment.

Most researchers would agree that a mission statement should be concise—free from unnecessary elaboration. If the mission statement is less than twenty-five words, it becomes more a motto than a mission statement. Conversely, a mission described in more than three or four pages means that management has not come to grips with its priorities and fundamental issues. The best-worded mission statements are simple and to the point; they speak loudly and clearly, generate enthusiasm for the company's future, and elicit personal effort and dedication from everyone in the organization.

The mission statement should be clear and understandable—especially to employees—and should be brief enough for most people to keep in mind. It should clearly specify what business the organization is in, what customer or client needs the organization is attempting to meet, who the organization's primary customers or clients are, and how the organization plans to go about its business.

There are three distinct aspects to forming a well-conceived strategic vision and expressing it in a company mission statement.

1. Understanding what business the company is in
   (A company's business is defined by what needs it is trying to satisfy, by which customer groups it is targeting, and by the technologies it will use and the functions it will perform in serving the target market.)

2. Communicating the vision and mission in ways that are clear, concise, exciting and inspiring
3. Deciding when to alter the company's strategic course and change its business mission[7]

The Need for an Explicit Mission Statement

The mission statement should be a statement of fact. Ferrari's mission statement could be, "We build the best world-class race cars." Microsoft's could be, "We make the world's best software products." Characteristically it is a statement, not of measurable targets but of attitude, outlook, and orientation. The mission statement is a message designed to be inclusive of the expectations of all stakeholders in the company's performance over the long run. Many researchers agree that one method of developing the mission statement can be best understood by thinking about the business when it first began. What was it started for? What did the company intend to do? The typical business begins with the beliefs, desires, and aspirations of a single entrepreneur or a group of individuals with a common goal. Usually that sense of mission is based on several fundamentals.

1. The product or service of the business was intended to provide benefits at least equal to its price.
2. The product or service was intended to satisfy a customer need in a specific market that was not being met adequately.
3. The technology used in production was intended to provide a cost-competitive product or service.
4. The business was not only to survive but also to grow and be profitable.
5. The management philosophy was to result in a favorable public image and to provide financial and psychological rewards.
6. The functions of the business were to be communicated to and adopted by employees and stockholders.

Recent Developments in Mission Statements

Recently, three issues have become prominent in strategic planning and are increasingly addressed in development of and revisions to mission statements: sensitivity to consumer wants, concern for quality, and statements of company vision.[8]

1. Customers

"The customer is our top priority" is a slogan—in some form or other—used by the majority of businesses. Company focus on customer satisfaction helps its managers realize the importance of providing quality customer service. Strong customer service initiatives have enabled some firms to gain competitive advantage in the marketplace. Hence, many corporations make the customer service initiative a key component of their corporate mission.

2. Quality

"Quality is job 1!" This was a rallying cry not only for Ford Motor Corporation in the 1980s, but for many resurging U.S. businesses as well. Two U.S. management experts fostered a worldwide emphasis on quality in manufacturing. W. Edwards Deming's and J. M. Juran's messages were first embraced by Japanese managers, whose new quality consciousness led to global dominance in several industries including automobile, television, audio equipment, and electronic components. Deming summarizes his approach in fourteen now well-known points:

- Create constancy of purpose.
- Adopt the new philosophy.
- Cease dependence on mass inspection to achieve quality.
- End the practice of awarding business on price tag alone. Instead, minimize total cost, often by working with a single supplier.
- Improve constantly the system of production and service.
- Institute on-the-job training.
- Adopt and institute leadership.
- Drive out fear.
- Break down barriers between departments.
- Eliminate slogans, exhortations, and numerical targets.
- Eliminate numerical quotas and management by objective.
- Remove barriers that rob workers, engineers, and managers of their pride of workmanship.
- Institute a vigorous program of education and self-improvement.
- Put everyone in the company to work to accomplish the transformation.[9]

3. Vision Statement

Increasingly, employees desire to know where the company is, where the company wants to go, and how the company intends to get there. Importantly, employees today want to know how they can contribute to achieving the company's goals and objectives. So, many companies are now moving towards incorporating their vision into their mission statements.

Mission Statement Guidelines

The Guidelines for preparing relevant and meaningful mission statements should prove helpful to all members of the planning team. However the list serves only as a checklist and is not all-inclusive. Additional items may be needed depending on the complexity and scope of the company.

1. The mission statement is clear and understandable, especially to rank-and-file employees.
2. The mission statement is brief enough for most people to keep it in mind.
3. The mission statement clearly specifies what business the organization is in. This includes clear sentences about:

    *   What customer or client needs the organization is attempting to fill
    *   Who the organization's primary customers or clients are
    *   How the organization plans to go about its business

4. The mission statement should focus primarily on a single strategic thrust.
5. The mission statement should reflect the distinctive competence of the organization.
6. The mission statement should be broad enough to allow flexibility in implementation but not so broad as to lack focus.
7. The mission statement should serve as a template that managers and others in the organization can use in making decisions.
8. The mission statement must reflect the values, beliefs, and philosophy of operations of the organization as well as of the organizational culture.
9. The mission statement should reflect attainable goals.

10. The mission statement should be worded so that it serves as an energy source and rallying point for the organization.

Notes

1. Mary Coulter, *Strategic Management in Action,* 3rd edition, (Upper Saddle River, New Jersey: Pearson Education, 2005), 46-48.

2. Charles W. L. Hill and Gareth R. Jones, *Strategic Management Theory,* 7th ed., (New York: Houghton Mifflin Company, 2007), 16.

3. Arthur A. Thompson, Jr. and A. J. Strickland III, *Strategic Management: Concepts and Cases,* 12th ed., (Chicago: McGraw Hill Companies, 2001), 28.

4. Thompson and Strickland, *Strategic Management*, 7.

5. Mary Coulter, *Strategic Management*, 48.

6. Hill and Jones, *Strategic Management*, 13.

7. Thompson and Strickland, *Strategic Management*, 23.

8. John A. Pearce II and Richard B. Robinson, *Strategic Management*, (New York: McGraw Hill, 2007), 32-34.

9. Mary Walton, *The Deming Management Method*, (New York: The Putnam Publishing Group, 1986), 55-86.

Chapter 6

Organizational Systems Analysis: Analysis and Assessment

In this part of the strategic planning process, the planning team begins to dig deep into company operations, including what impacts the company from external forces as well as internal forces. The total assessment considers what the company does well and what its weaknesses are. It includes a thorough evaluation of company operations, workforce strengths and weaknesses, customer requirements, business opportunities, and inhibitors that may distract the company from achieving its vision and goals.

The first part of this overall assessment of the company situation begins with an input and output analysis. Every standard work on this subject proposes some form of analysis of company operations as a prelude to development of the strategic plan. Some lump the individual elements into something called a Situation Audit.[1] Mary Coulter describes this process in terms familiar to proponents of the SWOT process and presents them in two chapters of her book.[2] Thompson and Strickland also stress the importance of an assessment of the company operations and describe it as "evaluating company resources and competitive capabilities."[3] No matter which type of assessment works better for your company, each author recommends a formal, in-depth analysis of company operations, including the internal and external factors that impact the company's ability to function and perform effectively. Presented below are the elements of the Organization Systems Analysis (OSA) that accomplish this evaluation of company operations.

Input/Output Analysis

The Input/Output (I/O) Analysis is a tool to help planners develop a formal, in-depth systematic view of the organization and to identify and analyze every company input and output. It involves systematic identification, examination and assessment of everything that comes into the organization and everything that goes out of it. Typically inputs and outputs are as varied as products, piece parts, people, items supplied by suppliers, technical and engineering support, influence or direction from a parent organization, support services, administration, and so on.

The I/O analysis carefully examines roles and responsibilities of managers, their functions and responsibilities. It can be used to resolve conflicts, eliminate redundancy in operations, and serve to improve lines of communication. It defines program objectives/deliverables, work breakdown structures, master schedules, and actual processes. Other uses include defining prime and support responsibilities, defining each team member's role, and implementing ideas for improvement.

The list below shows only a few of the inputs or outputs that can be identified. Each organization will be different and have distinctive inputs and outputs, some more complex than others.

- Corporate goals, objectives or directives that may be imposed on your organization from a parent organization
- Commercial hardware or software needed in the production or service provided
- Business opportunities, both planned and unplanned
- Statements of work or work breakdown schedules imposed by customers
- Corporate policies & procedures
- Internal research and development requirements
- Technology advancements
- Customer requirements and customer specifications for products
- Support services such as finance and accounting, safety and security
- Changes in the global marketplace
- Finances/budgets
- Support services provided to customers
- Products/end items/systems

- Studies/analyses provided to customers
- Technical evaluations
- Plans/procedures
- Program documentation
- Program/system training

Roadblocks

Roadblocks are things that impede achievement of the strategic vision or attainment of the company goals. They include factors that inhibit quality, productivity, improvement of performance, or diminish efficiency and effectiveness. Roadblocks are variously defined as things the company does poorly or disadvantages the company has that prevent it from performing effectively in the marketplace. They can be internal or external processes, an organizational default, or existing procedures/policies that prevent the organization from achieving vision and goals. Management must try to identify all of the things that could happen that would keep the company from achieving its vision and goals.

In the SWOT process, roadblocks can be either threats or weaknesses, but in the OSA process roadblocks are considered as a separate entity. All roadblocks identified by the planning team should be considered and reviewed for significance. Some examples of roadblocks are shown in the list below.

- Corporate mentality against "new ideas," resistance to changing the organization, desire to keep the status quo
- Profit levels that do not permit allocation of resources for strategic planning
- Poor planning training
- Poor internal communication
- Poor staffing procedures (not readily responsive to needs)
- Insufficient training for employees to work at the levels needed to meet customer requirements
- Organizational structure that discourages an integrated approach
- Management with conflicting priorities
- "Rice bowl" mentality
- Disjointed interaction between operating units
- Absence of an employee reward system

- Unclear relationship between awards and achievements
- Poor understanding of customer service
- No capital investment to acquire hardware/software to do the job
- Lack of information resources library for employees to use in job performance
- Restriction of business opportunities, unwillingness to pursue new business opportunities
- Inadequate corporate support to meet marketplace competition
- Lack of easy access to and understanding of corporate policies and procedures
- Inadequate marketing resources and support
- Eroded technical support personnel
- Lack of sufficient back-up personnel/managers
- Hesitation in getting rid of dead wood

Internal and External Strength Analysis

The Internal and External Strength Analysis evaluates what the company does well and what its weaknesses are. In this evaluation, the planning team considers: 1) whether the company has an experienced, qualified workforce; 2) whether the company is known for quality products and services; 3) whether the company's budget permits adequate financing to begin and finish manufacture of quality products; and 4) whether the company's marketing department has sufficient resources to function in the global economy. Obviously there can be many more elements of the company operations that could be considered but the list above provides examples. There are many questions to be addressed in this section of the plan and they all require in-depth analysis and assessment of the company operations. Of course, each company is different and will have different strengths and weaknesses. Each company must identify and evaluate its own particular strengths and weaknesses and determine how they impact the company's ability to achieve its vision and attain its goals.

In the SWOT process, internal and external strengths are combined under the strengths category, but in OSA each element is considered separately. Examples of internal and external strengths include:

- Good technically competent managers and personnel
- Excellent training on planning and development of plans
- Excellent customer rapport
- History of delivering products on time and at cost
- Ability to staff up during peak work loads
- Sufficient business development funding and support
- Participative management style already in place
- Ideally suited for your market niche
- Workforce stability
- Internal training programs focused on improving employee performance

Competitive Analysis

Competitive analysis serves to identify and evaluate the company's current and potential competitors. As the marketplace continues to evolve into a more global economy, competitive analysis becomes even more important for survival. The leadership of the organization must completely understand what competitors are doing, how they are organized, how they control costs and still provide quality products and services, and also what their customers are saying. Some companies involved in mergers and acquisitions have improved their ability to compete in the global marketplace and are, therefore, more involved in the global economy. Mary Coulter dedicates an entire chapter to competitive analysis, demonstrating the importance of thoroughly analyzing the competition and assessing the global marketplace and the economic conditions driving the global economy including the global workforce.[4] Thompson and Strickland also stress the importance of performing a thorough competitive analysis by dedicating an entire chapter of their 12th edition to this process.[5] Suffice it to say, a strategic plan cannot be completed without an assessment of the competitive nature of the marketplace and an evaluation of what the competition is doing and how that impacts on the organization. There are several important questions to answer and variables to consider:

1. How do other firms define the scope of their market? The more similar their definitions, the more likely the firms will view each other as competitors.

2. How similar are the benefits the customers derive from the products and services that other firms offer? The more similar the benefits of products or services, the higher the level of substitutability between them. High substitutability levels force firms to compete fiercely for customers.
3. How committed are other firms to the industry? Although this question may appear to be far removed from the identification of competitors, it is in fact one of the most important questions that competitive analysis must address, because it sheds light on their long-term intentions and goals.
4. How trustworthy is the firm's intelligence about its competitors? To size up the commitment of potential competitors to the industry, reliable intelligence data are needed. Such data may shape potential resource commitments.

Common Mistakes in Analyzing Competitors

Identifying competitors is only one step in this analysis. The larger task becomes one of thoroughly understanding their position and their corporate strategy. It is a process laden with uncertainty and risk—a process in which executives sometimes make costly mistakes.

Examples of these mistakes are:

1. Overemphasizing current and known competitors while giving inadequate attention to potential entrants
2. Overemphasizing large competitors while ignoring small ones
3. Overlooking potential international competitors
4. Assuming that competitors will continue to behave in the same way they have behaved in the past
5. Misreading signals that may indicate a shift in the focus of competitors or a refinement of their present strategies or tactics
6. Overemphasizing competitors' financial resources, market position, and strategies while ignoring their intangible assets, such as a top management team
7. Assuming that all of the firms in the industry are subject to the same constraints or are open to the same opportunities
8. Believing that the purpose of strategy is to outsmart the competition, rather than to satisfy customer needs and expectations

Strategic Planning Assumptions

Strategic Planning Assumptions answer the 'What if ' question. What if our best customer goes to another source? What if our funding goes away? What if the union strikes? What if several of our top managers leave and go to another company? Answers to these and other similar questions can help planners to prepare for development of strategic goals. The assumptions made in this process provide the entire planning team with the same outlook for the future. In this step of strategic plan development, assumptions must be made relative to the roadblocks, internal strengths, and external opportunities that were identified previously and are important to the planning process.

Planning assumptions may include the following:

1. Crystal-ball gazing about the marketplace, funding levels, direction that technology is moving, and so on
2. Educated guesses about the future environment the organization will operate in and what will be affected
3. Things that the team expects to happen in the future that the team should take into account in developing their plan
4. Educated guesses about anything of importance and certainty concerning the future of the organization

This process converts the previously-gathered data into specific planning assumptions, all of which can have a dramatic influence on the results. The assumptions are the baseline from which the strategic plan will be developed; they must be clearly understood by everyone.

Completion of strategic planning assumptions signals the end of that element of the OSA and we are ready to move forward in the process to development of strategic goals and tactical objectives. However, before we move on, it is worth taking a look at a more traditional approach.

SWOT Analysis: A Traditional Approach to Internal Analysis

For some organizations, the OSA can simply be too costly in terms of time and resources. While the OSA conducts a formal assessment of each element comprising the strategic planning process, the SWOT process combines several of the elements into a single consideration and therefore can be a less expensive alternative. SWOT analysis is a historically popular technique through which managers create a quick overview of a company's strategic situation. SWOT is based on the assumption that an effective strategy derives from a good balance between a firm's internal and external resources (strengths and weaknesses) and its internal and external situation (opportunities and threats). A good strategic plan would then maximize a company's strengths and opportunities and minimizes its weaknesses and threats. Accurately applied, this simple process has sound, insightful implications for the design of a successful strategy, is less expensive than the Organizational System Analysis, and may suffice in many cases in lieu of the OSA.

Using SWOT Analysis in Strategic Analysis

SWOT analysis is most commonly used as a logical framework to guide discussion and reflection about a firm's situation and basic alternatives. Used in planning sessions, the SWOT analysis framework serves to give focus to discussion of those factors. In a series of planning group discussions, what one manager sees as an opportunity, another may see as a potential threat. Likewise, a strength to one manager may be seen as a weakness by another. The SWOT framework provides an organized basis for insightful discussion and information sharing, which may improve the quality of choices and decisions managers subsequently make.

Limitations of SWOT Analysis

SWOT analysis has been the framework of choice among many managers for a long time because of its simplicity and its emphasis on sound strategy formulation. But SWOT analysis is a broad conceptual approach, making it susceptible to certain key limitations.

In summary, SWOT analysis has long been a traditional approach to internal and external analysis of an organization. It offers a generalized effort to examine internal capabilities in light of external factors, and can be as detailed as planners desire, especially with respect to key opportunities and threats. SWOT Analysis has limitations that must be recognized if it is to be the basis for any firm's strategic decision-making process.

Notes

1. George A. Steiner, *A Step-by-Step Guide to Strategic Planning*, (New York: The Free Press, 1979), 122.

2. Mary Coulter, *Strategic Management in Action,* 3rd ed., (Upper Saddle River, New Jersey: Pearson Education Inc., 2005), 65-135.

3. Thompson and Strickland, *Strategic Management: Concepts and Cases*, 12th ed., (New York, McGraw Hill Companies, 2001), 17-125.

4. Mary Coulter, 148-194.

5. Thompson and Strickland, 117-125.

Chapter 7

Organizational Systems Analysis: Strategic Goals and Tactical Objectives

At this point in the development of the strategic plan, major goals and objectives must be developed. Once the organizational systems analysis is completed, the planning team is ready to begin formulating strategic goals. Strategic goals give direction to the long-range plans for achieving the vision of the company. These goals and objectives indicate where the company is headed and what the company wants to achieve. Strategic goals are designed to be achieved in a specific period of time. For example, a strategic goal could be written to indicate that it is to be reached within the next five years.

Unlike an aspiration or a hope, a strategic goal is always specific and realistic. A familiar example—one of the strategic goals for President Kennedy early in his presidency was to have a man on the moon by 1970. This goal was sufficiently long-range, had a specific time by which it had to be accomplished, and reflected a vision of what was to come. Strategic goals are management's commitment to achieve specific performance targets by a definite time.[1]

Medium-range goals mark the steps necessary to reach strategic goals. They are translated into more immediate targets called *tactical* objectives—ones that must be achieved over the next year or two to ensure that each strategic goal is accomplished. There may be several tactical objectives for each strategic goal. In this respect, the process of setting goals and objectives is very similar to project planning where significant events are labeled milestones and all the steps or actions leading to accomplishment of the milestone are called "inch pebbles." A strategic goal can be similar to a milestone whereas the tactical objective is more like an "inch pebble."

Thompson and Strickland stress the importance of setting strategic goals—which they call *long term objectives*.[2] "Setting objectives converts the strategic vision and directional course of action into target outcomes and performance milestones. Long term objectives represent a managerial commitment to producing specified results in a specified time frame." In other words, they spell out what has to be done and by when. Thompson and Strickland go further in requiring that long term objectives—or strategic goals, using the terms described in this document—must be both quantifiable and time-constrained.

Hill and Jones indicate that a strategic goal is precise and measurable in a future state of the company and reflects what a company must do to achieve its mission or vision. They go on to describe four main characteristics of a strategic goal.

1. The goal must be precise and measureable.
2. The goal must address crucial issues and therefore should not be an endless list of lesser issues within the company.
3. The goal must be challenging but realistic so that all employees can see achievement of the goal as challenging but achievable.
4. The goal must have a specific time period so that employees realize that the goal must be achieved by a given date and therefore everyone has a sense of urgency to attain the goal.[3]

Pearce and Robinson describe seven criteria that can be used to evaluate strategic goals. They must be flexible, measurable over time, motivating, suitable, understandable, and achievable. Each of the seven is related both to the workforce and to management. Obviously, the criteria are intended to result in realistic, achievable, and verifiable goals that motivate everyone to work towards their achievement within the time frame specified.[4]

Setting Strategic Goals

To begin development of the strategic plan, top management, along with the planning team, determines exactly what is to be accomplished in the next three to five years in moving the organization toward its vision. This identification of specific milestones to be reached makes it possible to evaluate progress toward attaining the vision. As we have seen from the research, setting strategic goals converts the strategic vision into target outcomes and performance milestones. It represents management's determination to produce specific results within a specified time frame. Reaching strategic goals requires spelling out exactly what is to be done, by whom, and when. Experience shows that managers who set strategic goals for each key result area and act aggressively to achieve their performance targets, typically outperform managers that only have good intentions.[5]

The terms *strategic goals* and *tactical objectives* are each used to convey a special meaning, with strategic goals being the less specific but more encompassing concept. Research indicates that most authors accept this distinction. The point to remember is that strategic goals are longer range and more conceptual whereas tactical objectives are more focused and to the point. Tactical objectives are those specific shorter-range actions that must take place in order to complete or achieve the strategic goal. A strategic goal may require many tactical objectives for its completion.

During the planning process, the planning team will generate a number of strategic goals intended to achieve the vision. Essentially, strategic goals should result in moving the company from where it is to where it wants to go, making it what it wants to be, and focusing on achievement of management's vision. The planning team must consider what the organization must accomplish in the next five years to achieve its vision. As part of the process to develop strategic goals, the planning team considers certain elements to assure the strategic goal is focused on the vision. Strategic goal development has several components.

1. The specific actions needed to accomplish the vision
2. Development of a prioritized list of strategic goals—Available resources and fiscal constraints will dictate how many of the strategic goals can be accomplished within the schedule imposed by top management.
3. Evaluation of each strategic goal in the light of the organization's vision and mission statements, roadblocks that were considered, and any strategic planning assumptions

Strategic planners commonly establish strategic goals in six areas.[6] There may be more or less depending on the size and complexity of the organization, but these six serve as an example of the areas of the organization that can be considered for developing strategic goals.

1. *Profitability*—The ability of any firm to operate in the long run depends on its attaining an acceptable level of profits.
2. *Productivity*—Strategic managers constantly try to increase the productivity of their systems.
3. *Competitive Position*—One measure of corporate success is relative dominance in the marketplace, often using total sales or market share as measures of their competitive position.
4. *Employee Development*—Employees value education and training, in part because they lead to increased compensation and job security.
5. *Employee Relations*—Managers promote good employee relations by recognizing employee needs and expectations, recognizing their loyalty, showing interest in their welfare through safety programs, and by arranging for worker representation on management committees and participation in stock option plans.
6. *Technological Leadership*—Companies must decide whether to lead or follow in the marketplace since each requires a different strategic posture.

Tactical Objectives

An organization needs both long-range strategic goals and more immediate, medium- or short-range tactical objectives. Typically, tactical objectives involve short-range, specific, step-by-step actions to reach a strategic goal. Tactical objectives determine the immediate and near-term actions than must be taken and indicate the speed at which management wants the organization to progress, as well as the level of performance desired over the next one or two years. Tactical objectives should be challenging but achievable and generally follow the same criteria we saw earlier for strategic goals.

Components of Tactical Objectives

All activities to this point have been in preparation for developing tactical objectives. The planning team should consider the vision, mission, roadblocks, strategic goals, and all the other components of the OSA previously developed. A potential danger with developing a list of tactical objectives for each strategic goal is overload. While some organizations are not overloaded by this approach, the resource requirements for its coordination and implementation are more intense. Obviously the more strategic goals and supporting tactical objectives that are identified, the more company resources and funding must be allocated to their achievement.

In one approach, the top-ranked tactical objectives are held beside the top-ranked strategic goals. If a strategic goal is identified with no tactical objectives supporting it, that particular goal should be reviewed to determine if it is really needed. It could be that nothing can be done during the next two years toward accomplishing that strategic goal. This situation requires a decision whether to set an additional tactical objective or to reconsider the strategic goal. Similarly, when a tactical objective is found that does not support any of the strategic goals, planners must determine whether a strategic goal is missing, or if this tactical objective is something that should not presently be included.

Notes

1. Patrick J. Montana and Bruce H. Charnov, *Management*, 3d ed., (New York: Barron's, 2000), 108.
2. Thompson and Strickland, 12th ed., 30.
3. Hill Jones, 17.
4. John A. Pierce and Richard B. Robinson, *Strategic Management*, (New York: McGraw Hill, 2007), 192-93.
5. Thompson and Strickland, 9th ed., 30.
6. Data reflected in items 1-6 were gathered from: Hill and Jones, 17, 18, 132, 421; Mary Coulter, 48, 124; and Thompson and Strickland, 12th ed., 41-48.

Chapter 8

Implementing the Strategic Plan

Once the plan has been approved and the planning team has converted the results of the OSA or SWOT analysis into actionable items and has prioritized the strategic goals and tactical objectives, it is time to publish the strategic plan and prepare for implementation. Part of this process includes development of detailed actions to implement the plan and to allocate funding and resources to complete each tactical objective. Accomplishing every tactical objective is the key (basic) to achieving the strategic goals and is the essential link between planning and effective implementation. Since there are many books, papers, dissertations and other forms of professional literature on implementation of strategy within an organization, it is not the intent of the author to replicate this library of information. However, a few descriptions and definitions are in order to provide students with a basic knowledge of implementation strategy in an organizational setting.

Coulter defines strategy implementation as putting the organization's various strategies into action by utilizing the organization's resources, capabilities, and core competencies to play a significant role in implementing competitive strategy.[1] Hill and Jones expand on the Coulter definition a bit by describing strategy implementation as putting strategies into action by designing, delivering, and supporting products, improving the efficiency and effectiveness of operations, and designing a company's organizational structure, control systems and processes to execute the vision and become the new organization of the future.[2] For our third source, we turn to the Thompson and Strickland definition and description of strategy implementation. They describe strategy implementation as consisting of seven elements.[3]

1. Building an organization capable of carrying out the strategy
2. Developing budgets that reflect the actions needed to be accomplished
3. Establishing supportive policies and procedures that enable the tasks to be completed
4. Motivating the workforce including managers in ways that induce them to complete action items that further the strategic plan
5. Tying the organization reward system to achievement of action items as part of the strategic plan
6. Creating a company culture that facilitates carrying out the plans and actions necessary to implement the plan and attain the goals and objectives
7. Creating the best practices and programs that facilitate continuous improvement and enable the organization to continue to achieve its strategic vision

All research indicates that without effective implementation of the strategic plan, the document becomes a dust-gathering publication on the shelf of the organization's managers. Implementation is essential to the strategic planning process. Action items necessary to accomplish tactical objectives and attain strategic goals must be effectively executed. Such implementation at each level of the plan is essential to turning the organization's vision into a reality and moving the company from the here and now into its future.

Some Preliminaries

Before the actual execution of the plan, steps must be taken to ensure that its implementation process goes smoothly. One popular method of implementing the parts of the plan is to create process action teams of three to five people—more or less depending on the complexity of the organization and of the tasks to be accomplished—to develop scoping (feasibility) proposals. These teams typically are made up of the members of the planning team who developed the plan, frequently supplemented by staff and lower level managers and employees. They are given a deadline to develop a scoping proposal for their respective action item. The table below depicts some items to be considered in a scoping proposal.

Table 8-1
Scoping Proposals[4]

What Has To Be Done?
Who Has To Be Involved?
When Should Activities Begin?
How Should The Project Be Implemented?
What Are The Associated Costs And Benefits?
What Are The Measures Of Success?

A completed scoping proposal should be fewer than five pages in length—again depending on the complexity of the organization and the action items to be accomplished—and should, in effect scope out exactly what needs to be accomplished in order to complete that particular action. Many organizations incorporate a review and evaluation process in this step. Scoping proposals are normally reviewed by a management-appointed committee composed of members of the planning team to determine the resources needed to accomplish the action items. Once a plan has the approval of its scoping team, a group is formed for its implementation.

Since implementation planning is designed to determine how to proceed with implementation of the tactical objectives, the planning team should identify which tactical objectives are currently being worked on, and which of them have shown no progress. This of course assumes it is not the first year of implementing the strategic plan, in which case all tactical objectives would be new.

An accountability matrix is a useful tool for assigning tactical objectives. One example of a successful accountability matrix is in the form of a MS Word table. In this example, all the tactical objectives are listed in rows and columns are headed: Tactical Objectives, Status, Actions Needed, Process Action Team Lead, and Next Review Date.

Table 8-2
Sample Process Action Matrix[5]

Tactical Objective	Status = on-going or completed	Actions Needed	Process Action Team Lead	Next Review Date

Experience has shown that the same individuals should not serve on more than one action team; otherwise, they may become overextended. Remember, the action team is an *ad hoc* assignment over and above each team member's everyday job. Assignment of accountability for a tactical objective does not imply that those assigned must personally implement the objective. Rather, it means they are accountable for managing the implementation.

The next task is development of an action plan for each tactical objective. Every tactical objective assigned to an action team requires an action plan. Complexity of the objective may be the deciding factor. When the agenda allows, draft action plans are developed and presented during the planning session. If not, the teams are given a deadline to have their action plans ready. At the latest, action plans should be ready at the first quarterly planning review.

Putting a strategy into place and getting the organization to execute it effectively is a formidable task. Implementing strategy is primarily an operations-driven activity revolving around the management of people. While successful strategy *making* depends on business vision, careful and thorough internal and external examination of the company operations, competitive analysis, and entrepreneurial creativity, successful strategy *implementation* depends on leading, motivating, and working with others to assure that the strategy execution complements the way the organization performs its core business activities. Implementing a strategy is an action-oriented task that tests a manager's ability to: 1) direct organizational change 2) supervise business processes 3) motivate people and 4) achieve performance targets. Strategy implementation is fundamentally an action-oriented activity involving organizing, budgeting, policy-making, motivating, culture-building, and leading/supervising. The strategy implementer's task is to convert the strategic plan into action and get on with what needs to be done to achieve the targeted tactical objectives and strategic goals.[6]

Major Considerations

In order to begin development of the implementation plan, managers must have a clear grasp of the major tasks to be accomplished.

- The manager must consider an organization structure capable of carrying out the strategy successfully. Process action teams are one proven method of implementing overall objectives and goals.
- It is necessary to develop budgets ensuring that sufficient resources are available to successfully implement the strategy. Too often once the strategic plan is developed, top management discovers there is little or no funding identified to implement the strategy. This has a stifling effect on the planning team and the employees who have been waiting to see what happens after the planning is done, only to be told, "The plan is great, except we're not going to implement it because we didn't plan for the funding."
- Establishing the appropriate plans and policies must be done with the consent of the employees to get them to buy into the changes.
- Support systems must be established to enable organization personnel to carry out their strategic roles successfully. The old military principle holds true: "Don't give me the responsibility for a task without the requisite authority to carry it out."
- Rewards and incentives must be tied to the achievement of performance objectives and good strategy execution.
- A work environment and corporate culture must be fostered that supports the organization's strategic plan.
- Leaders must demonstrate the qualities needed to drive implementation forward in ongoing improvement.

Specific Actions to Proceed with Implementation Planning

At this point in the development of the strategic plan, it is imperative that action plans detailing how to proceed with the implementation be developed. There is a series of steps recommended in this process.

Selection of An Implementation Team

Putting together a strong management team with the right personal chemistry and mix of skills is the first strategy-implementing step. This will be the group of individuals given the responsibility to implement the strategy; they are the key players on the process action teams. They must have the foresight to see what needs to be done and how to get it done.

Often the task of implementing the strategic plan simply requires more time and energy than managers can dedicate to it when they are also tasked with day-to-day operations activities. In this case, a team is selected whose members are relieved from their normal daily activities so they can focus on developing the implementation plan. Six of the most frequently used team organizations are:

1. **Special project teams**
    These teams are separate, largely self-sufficient, work groups that oversee the completion of a special activity *e.g.*, setting up a new technological process, bringing out a new product, starting up a new venture, consummating a merger with another company, supervising the completion of a government contract, supervising the construction and opening of a new activity, or implementing new employee benefit or reward programs. Special project teams are especially suited for unique situations that have a limited time frame. They can benefit organizations that do not have personnel who can do such work in addition to regular duties.
2. **Cross-functional task forces**
    Here, a number of top level executives and/or specialists are brought together to solve problems requiring specialized expertise from several parts of the organization *e.g.*, to coordinate strategy-related activities that span departmental boundaries, or to explore ways to leverage the skills of different

functional specialists into broader core competencies. Cross-functional task forces seem to be more effective when: 1) they have fewer than ten members 2) membership is voluntary 3) the seniority of the members is proportional to the importance of the problem 4) the task force moves swiftly to completion of its assignment 5) they are used sparingly 6) no staff is assigned and 7) documentation is scant.

3. **Venture Teams**

   Venture Teams are composed of a newly-formed group of individuals who manage the launch of a specific new business. The difficulties with venture teams include: 1) deciding who the venture manager should report to 2) deciding whether funding for ventures should come from corporate, business or departmental budgets 3) managing to keep the venture clear of bureaucratic and vested interests and 4) coordination of a large number of different ventures.

4. **Self-contained work teams**

   These groups are composed of individuals drawn from different disciplines, who work together on a semi-permanent basis to continuously improve organizational performance in specific strategy-related areas. The only difference between these groups and special project teams is their duration.

5. **Process action teams**

   These teams are composed of functional specialists who perform pieces of a business process together on a team instead of assigning them to their home-base functional department. Such teams can be empowered to re-engineer the process, held accountable for results, and rewarded on the basis of how well the process is performed. These teams normally work in close harmony with strategic goals and tactical objectives.

6. **Contact managers**

   These are individuals who serve as single points of contact for customers when the steps of a process either are so complex or are dispersed in such a way that integrating them for a team to perform is impractical. The best results are achieved when contact managers are empowered to use their own judgment to get things done in a manner that will please customers.[7]

Preparation of the Implementation Plan

While each organization's implementation plan will be different, it is appropriate to provide an example for students to see what normally is included in an implementation plan. Obviously, as the complexity of the organization increases the implementation plan will also increase in complexity and detail. A typical implementation plan, no matter what the format, should list each tactical objective, the actions needed to complete that tactical objective, the current status, the person selected to lead this effort, and the ongoing activity. Normally, the implementation plan details any corrective actions that are to be taken, indicates additional resources that may be needed, and identifies any subordinate action plan that may need to be developed.

Summary

For summary of implementation planning and execution we turn to George Steiner's book *Strategic Planning: What Every Manager Must Know*.[8] His summary statement is very much to the point, "No company ever made a nickel of profit by making plans: the profit comes from the implementation of the plans." The objective of strategic planning and management is to successfully and effectively create and implement superior strategies that will take the company from the here and now into the future. Steiner describes the process of implementation as one of developing tactical plans and objectives and then creating the budgets that permit managers to efficiently carry them out. Such short-range plans and objectives must be realistic and achievable within the time frames developed by the planners.

Notes

1. Coulter, 8.
2. Hill and Jones, 3, 20.
3. Thompson and Strickland, 9th ed., 11-14.
4. The information reflected in this table represents data collected and synopsized by Dr. Bertocci from many sources, but primarily, Thompson and Strickland, 9th and 12th eds.; Coulter; and Hill and Jones.

5. This table represents a rudimentary matrix that can be used in implementation planning. Many other formats can also be used for this purpose as long as they provide the check and balance systems for managers to use in implementation of the plan objectives and goals.

6. Thompson and Strickland, 12th ed. 241.

7. Thompson and Strickland, 12th ed. 266, 267.

8. Steiner, 21, 213, 215.

Chapter 9

The Next Steps

So what happens next? Are we done? Once the strategic plan has been developed and implementation planning is well underway, what happens next in the organization? What are the next steps to ensure the organization remains in the growing, planning mode? A few more popular ones can be found in the table below.

- Continue working on the action plans for all tactical objectives. Another meeting should be scheduled as a working meeting to review action plans that have been developed.
- Once the action plans are reviewed and agreed upon by the management team, a small group should then use the output developed in the strategic planning session to assemble the entire strategic plan which is then published after review by the management team.
- Implement the action plans.
- Schedule quarterly review sessions as a means of getting the management team together on a regular basis to discuss implementation issues and report on progress.

Project Management

Project management is both a science and an art. However, the art, the skill, and the discipline associated with this step of performance improvement are far more important than any specific project management technique. Effective project management, as experienced managers know, requires attention to detail, a balance of impatience and patience, persistence, consistency, discipline, communication, and coordination, in addition to the application of appropriate techniques.

This is the action step. It consists of organizing, executing, measuring, and evaluating. Those assigned to the implementation of tactical objectives are expected to self-manage that process. They should seek help or approval as needed; they can bring others onto the project, but they must remain involved. Complete delegation of a tactical objective to someone not involved in developing the tactical objectives is ineffective and not recommended.

At the first planning review meeting, the individual or group will be expected to report on progress. Researchers of management theory tell us that in most cases the things that get accomplished correctly and in a timely manner are the things that managers check on.

Measurement and Evaluation

Top management must have a way to know that the strategic plan is working. This phase of the process involves daily measurement, assessment, and evaluation of the impact of strategic and tactical objectives on organizational system performance. Planning team members are held accountable for tracking implementation progress and for measuring its impact using new or existing measurement systems. Many organizations develop a visibility room for displaying these measures. This step continues throughout the first year and provides data for repeating the process the following year. All organizations have some form of measurement system, no matter how informal or incomplete.

Managing Effective Implementation/Review and Continual Evolution

Continuous support from management and a visible tracking system will help ensure effective implementation. Quarterly review meetings will help track and review progress, update the plan, and identify ways to improve the process. They are an excellent way to ensure continued application of the strategic planning process throughout the year. Their purpose is broader than implementation of tactical objectives. They also facilitate sharing of information, review and evaluation of progress, and promotion of improved implementation.

At one of the management reviews, top management should begin preparing for the next planning cycle. After all, the marketplace has changed since the last strategic plan, some competitors have merged, and customers want things still better, cheaper, and faster. The company needs to change in order to continue to compete in the ever-changing market place. Companies should not be constrained by the previous year's planning work. Many organizations use the review periods as a time to expand participation by inviting more participants to the planning team from all levels in the organization. The process is refined to fit the organization and to become ingrained in the way business is conducted. Similar considerations are taken into account once again: how the marketplace has changed; how well the competition is doing compared to the company being reviewed; and what the company now needs to do to survive in a dynamic global economy. It is a process of metamorphosis in which the organization must constantly evolve to adjust to its changing environment.

Chapter 10

Findings and Conclusions

Our study of strategic planning and management finds that concepts of strategic planning are continually changing as the business marketplace changes and new aggressive competition surfaces. Based on the research and material gathered from various sources, the evolving nature of strategic planning and management is well documented. Trying to define exactly what comprises strategic planning and management and arrive at a neat package that describes all strategic planning is difficult for many reasons. Most importantly, we find that, as the circumstances that define strategic planning and management change, so do the concepts required to meet new challenges. Thus, as theories that describe and define strategic planning and management continue to evolve, no single theory occupies a definitive place or holds a dominant view. Yet, certain characteristics are common to most theories: 1) most researchers agree that for companies to survive some form of strategic planning and management must take place; 2) a vision that sets forth where the organization is, where the organization wants to go and how the organization is going to get there is essential for everyone in the organization to understand and accept the need for change; 3) change in the organization is difficult for many reasons presented in this book; and 4) resistance to change in the organization can be managed.

Thus, in our study of strategic planning and management, we note that the body of research supports two general findings. First, strategic planning is essential for coping with the changing global marketplace. Second, strategic planning and management is more than developing a set of overriding goals and objectives; it also includes successful implementation of action plans to accomplish the vision of the company.

As definitions of strategic planning and management have evolved, a consensus has emerged concerning how vital a vision is to strategic planning—a vision of where the organization is, where it wants to go and how it is going to get there. Mary Coulter[1] provides an interesting perspective on corporate leadership and the need for a vision. She describes corporate leadership as the ability to anticipate, envision, maintain flexibility, think strategically, and work with others in the organization to initiate changes that will create a viable and valuable future for the organization. Further she indicates that there are six key dimensions which are identified with setting the vision: determining the purpose of the organization; maintaining and exploiting core capabilities; developing human resources through expert recruitment and training; creating and sustaining strong organizational culture; emphasizing ethical decisions and practices; and establishing appropriately balanced controls. In essence, strategic planning is about survival in the global marketplace and taking a proactive approach to changing the organization to address the evolving business marketplace. Those that do this will thrive; those that don't, will struggle to survive.

Part one of the book presented the underlying principles and theory, examining strategic planning and management in organizational settings. Part two described a detailed approach to strategic planning featuring a modification of the approach by Thompson and Strickland that we titled the *participative approach*. The participative approach featured participation by top management with specific roles and responsibilities but also included participation of members of the organization from all levels. This approach facilitates developing support from the employees through the members of the planning team who represent various sections of the workforce. Lastly, the book discussed implementation of the plan. Without vigorous implementation of the goals and objectives, the strategic plan becomes just another book on the shelf of the CEO.

Note

1. Coulter, p. 14.

Bibliography

Below, Patrick J., George L. Morrisey, and Betty L. Acomb. *The Executive Guide to Strategic Planning*. San Francisco: Jossey-Bass, 1987.

Bennis, Warren G. and Burt Nanus. *Leaders—The Strategy for Taking Charge*. New York: Harper and Row, Harper Business Series, 1985.

Colby, Marvelle S. and Selig Alkon. *Introduction to Business*, New York: Harper Collins, 1991.

Coulter, Mary. *Strategic Management in Action,* 3d ed. Upper Saddle River, New Jersey: Pearson Education, 2005.

Deming, W. Edwards. *Out of the Crisis*. Cambridge, MA: The MIT Press, 1986.

Dunlap, Albert J. with Bob Andelman, *Mean Business: How I Save Bad Companies and Make Good Companies Great*. New York: Simon and Schuster/Fireside, 1997.

Hill, Charles W. L. and Gareth Jones. *Strategic Management Theory,* 7th ed. Boston: Houghton Mifflin, 2007.

Kirkpatrick, Shelly A and Edwin A. Locke. "Leadership: Do Traits Really Matter?" *Academy of Management Executives,* May 1991.

Kotter, John P. *What Leaders Really Do: Managing People and Organizations*. Boston: McGraw Hill, Harvard Business School Practice of Management Series, 1992.

Matteson, Michael T. and John M. Ivancevich, eds. *Management and Organizational Behavior Classics,* 7th ed. Boston: Irwin-McGraw Hill, 1999.

Montana, Patrick J. and Bruce H. Charnov. *Management*, 3d ed. New York: Barron's Management Series, 2000.

Pierce, John A. II and Richard B. Robinson. *Strategic Management*. New York: McGraw Hill, 2007.

Robert, Michel. *Strategy II—Pure and Simple*. New York: McGraw Hill, 1997.

Schilling, Melissa A. *Strategic Management of Technological Innovation,* 2d ed. New York: McGraw Hill-Irwin, 2008.

Steiner, George A. *Strategic Planning—What Every Manager Must Know*. New York: Simon and Schuster, The Free Press, 1997.

Thompson, Arthur A. and A. J. Strickland III. *Strategic Management: Concepts and Cases,* 9th ed. Chicago: Richard D. Irwin, 1996.

———. *Strategic Management: Concepts and Cases,* 10th ed. Chicago: Richard D. Irwin Company, 1997.

———. *Strategic Management: Concepts and Cases,* 12th ed. New York: Irwin-McGraw Hill, 2001.

Walton, Mary. *The Deming Management Method*. New York: Putnam Publishing Group, 1986.

Welch, Jack and John A. Byrne. *Jack: Straight from the Gut*. New York: Warner Business Books, 2001.

About the Author

David I. Bertocci is an Associate Professor at Kaplan University and has been teaching online distance-learning courses for over twelve years. After receiving his MS degree in Education/Counseling from Long Island University, Dr. Bertocci obtained his PhD in Business and Management from Capella University. In the course of his doctoral studies, he discovered the need for textbooks written for students in online programs—sufficiently explanatory and engaging texts, geared for working adults who do not have the advantage of direct classroom participation. This book is the second in a series of three specifically designed for online education courses in management, strategic planning. and leadership.

Dr. Bertocci is a former military officer who served in high-level planning positions throughout his military career. Following his retirement from the military, he worked for several companies in the defense industry before starting his own. Each assignment provided the opportunity for development of strategic plans, and strategic management. Early in his career working in industry, he was instrumental in training and facilitating strategic planning for several offices within the Department of Defense. In 1995, he started his own engineering and technical support company to provide planning and management services for that agency. As part of that work, he helped develop strategic plans and facilitated strategic planning sessions for several organizations. Two of his major contributions were the Strategic Plan and Planning Sessions for a US Navy air program office and a strategic plan for a joint services office.

Having held planning positions in his military and business careers, Dr. Bertocci began teaching online courses in management, strategic planning, and leadership at several colleges and universities. This book reflects his experience in strategic planning and management positions as well as his teaching interests.